T0199164

Until He Sees Himself in Me

Basilel Woodside

WESTBOW
PRESS®
A DIVISION OF THOMAS NELSON
& ZONDERVAN

This book is a work of non-fiction. Unless otherwise noted, the author and the publisher make no explicit guarantees as to the accuracy of the information contained in this book and in some cases, names of people and places have been altered to protect their privacy.

Scripture taken from the King James Version of the Bible.

Scripture quotations taken from the Holy Bible, New Living Translation, Copyright © 1996, 2004. Used by permission of Tyndale House Publishers, Inc., Wheaton, Illinois 60189. All rights reserved.

WestBow Press books may be ordered through booksellers or by contacting:

WestBow Press
A Division of Thomas Nelson & Zondervan
1663 Liberty Drive
Bloomington, IN 47403
www.westbowpress.com
1 (866) 928-1240

Because of the dynamic nature of the Internet, any web addresses or links contained in this book may have changed since publication and may no longer be valid. The views expressed in this work are solely those of the author and do not necessarily reflect the views of the publisher, and the publisher hereby disclaims any responsibility for them.

Any people depicted in stock imagery provided by Thinkstock are models, and such images are being used for illustrative purposes only.
Certain stock imagery © Thinkstock.

ISBN: 978-1-5127-2117-1 (sc)
ISBN: 978-1-5127-2119-5 (hc)
ISBN: 978-1-5127-2118-8 (e)

Library of Congress Control Number: 2015919170

Print information available on the last page.

WestBow Press rev. date: 11/17/2015

Contents

Foreword

When I was a little boy, my father used to service his old outboard motor. When he was off from his regular job as a lumberjack, he would fill a fifty-five-gallon barrel with seawater and set up his motor on the rim so the shaft was inside. He'd start the motor and perform maintenance and adjustments while it ran. After he completed his work on the motor, he would race it at almost top speed for sometimes half an hour. No matter at what speed the motor ran, the barrel never tipped over; it never moved or ever even shook. Dad has gone to be with the Lord almost fifty years now, but I can still hear that old motor roaring in my mind.

Denominational doctrines are barrels with running motors; they're only clerical novelties that won't move you and certainly won't get you further along in your spiritual journey.

That outboard was a great way to explore the beautiful coast but only after it was attached to the stern of a boat. In the same way, dogmas by themselves won't give you the freedom and mobility you need to grow and explore spiritually. You may be very invested in and knowledgeable about your denomination, but whenever you explore the outer edges of your denomination, you'll discover that much of your treasure is trash.

Dear friend, God expects you and all Christian believers to grow, and that requires dispensing with traditions and doctrinal heresies. By the sincere truth of the gospel, seek to become one with Him until he sees Himself in you.

The reality is simple: church denominations are called that because they're the personal opinions of groups and subgroups that have strong ideas of what the Bible means. Many have contrived dogmas that have prompted some to label them as cults. These heretical beliefs are disastrous to the nature of the new creation. *Until He Sees Himself in Me* explores the spiritual possibilities in Jesus Christ and will help you reach maturity in your understanding of the Bible. This book is free of doctrinal biases and denominational dogmas. It will expose seekers to the truths in the doctrines of the Lord Jesus and the apostles. There is no reason to drink poison behind jungle-like walls as Jim Jones and his unfortunate followers did.

Just as my father's outboard motor created passionate but totally ineffectual wakes in a drum of greasy water, too often, too many good Christians with awesome God-given gifts and potentials are constrained by selfish people looking to monopolize their talents by chaining them to doctrines. This book will teach you who you should be, pinpoint where you are, offer my idea of what you can be, and offer you a clear road map of how to get there.

Many see sanctification as obedience to denominational rules, but the true sanctification is a cultivation of Christlikeness and image. To God be the glory.

Acknowledgments

The great and precious wealth of knowledge I gained through the research I conducted for this book has given me an infusion of life and a grasp of life's potential. My spirit has never been so alive and so desirous of becoming Christ like. I've connected to that river of living water that flows from Him. I give many thanks to a number of great and indispensable people.

I thank my wife, Paulette, who has been a cornucopia of resources, a constant source of support and help, and most of all, a friend whose inspirational encouragement has inspired me to see this work to its end. I thank her for her feedback, for proofing and editing this work, and for being a super sounding board. Her opinions have been the source of great insight for me.

Many thanks to the congregation of the Spiritual Counseling House of Our Lord Ministries for understanding when I seemed intolerable to people who wanted to settle for church traditions, and again thank you for your prayers and belief in my work. The value you have placed on my teaching has encouraged me. The Lord Jesus declared that we would do greater works than He did. Your confidence in this book's ability to evangelize the world has given me enthusiasm. I thank God for allowing me to be your pastor for twelve glorious years. God bless and make you prosperous.

Introduction

So much knowledge is so readily accessible today that it would seem conceited, even presumptuous, to suggest that no one has previously implemented the procedures of the doctrine of salvation in accordance with our Creator's will.

I have labored under extreme duress with so many inadequate thoughts and have been plagued by so many questions about salvation in my thirty-year walk with the Lord. I've sought answers only to be given frivolous, dead-end theories and no explanations. What I was taught left me in darkness with no real understanding of salvation even after fifty years of well-intentioned Christian living.

Likewise, many others have given up the struggle; they were bored and depressed by the rigidity of denominational dogmas. Many never discover the true purpose of God in the plan of salvation and are left unaware that they were called to a higher purpose.

As have so many others, I thought that the height and fruition of the Christian walk involved rote memorization of the Word of God and endeavoring to be as obedient as possible to church etiquette—the right tone of voice and a pleasant visage. These qualities are good but not sufficient, because they are shallow. I wanted to explore my faith's shallow splendors but more so the truth, which I was oblivious to. I'd never heard of the implementation of the gospel.

I learned that we would understand the real benefits of the gospel when we got to heaven and would grasp what Paul meant when he said, "We see through a glass darkly, now I know in part, but when that which is perfect that which is part would be done away with ..." 1 Corinthians 13:12 (KJV). I learned that it was wrong and ungodly to expect prosperity that being Christ-like would allow you to meet Him in the sky. God doesn't expect perfection; we couldn't become perfect anyway. Unconceivably, people I had held in the highest regard as role models couldn't believe beyond this idea. They based their beliefs on philosophical conclusions built on the understanding they gathered from "Now we see through a glass darkly but then ..." (1 Corinthians 12 KJV). They said, "Live on. We will understand it better by and by when we get to heaven."

That kind of Christianity brought me only momentary gratification, and then a crouching boredom began to stalk me. I met people everywhere who looked like everyone else, said the same things, and proudly showed off how anointed they were; they would get excited when their favorite Scripture was quoted, but they demonstrated no distinguishing spiritual characteristics nothing that would distinctly individualize them. They could not be told apart from others spiritually, most are encased in ego porticoes, except in places where they leave their physical appearance protruding. Their lipsticks are in coordinated moderation to the rest of their physical appearance which are most often mitigating. Most noticeable among these people was that they rattled off Scripture after Scripture as if that were the distinguishing hallmark of a devoted Christian. This glaring chasm may leave you dumbfounded for a while, but with all this pressing improbability, it is not difficult to see why.

I too had once been obsessed by these frivolous displays. In my early Christian life, I wrote Scriptures on my palm of my hand; I believed that was a way to grow spiritually. I thought. This seemed to be the way to go, and quite a big deal at that, supposedly, just any Dick or Jane could accurately rattle off long passages of especially on the spur of the moment. I thought then that this exemplified commitment and growth. Church leaders praised me for reciting the Scripture, and people stared at me, reading my lips for accuracy.

Many brilliant theologians and pastors in our universities and churches use the information highway to gather information on any perceivable topic and then offer it to their students and congregations. They have conducted assiduous research and have dissected the gospel. Nonetheless, something critical is missing from the lives of many Christians.

The moral fabric of our communities has degraded. Even with all the information available, people still seem predisposed to spiritual and physical weakness. The nature of our introspective mentality signals disturbing inadequacies and insufficiencies in our spiritual lives. We cannot pinpoint or access that extra something that should enhance our desires to want to be more.

This dramatic irony is playing out in a vicious fantasy called the pursuit of reality. Christians don't know or are too afraid to say they are seeking to become godlike. Jesus is God, they say, and no one could be like Him. This is the irony of fallacy. When acting only to imitate becomes the goal and not just a means, we deceive our psyches by pretending we're happy with whom we aren't happy. If we are to role-play, we expect the roles we take on to have some sort of transforming character.

It is taboo if not blasphemous to think of trying to be like God. "That's why Adam fell," they say. The Apostle John said, "As he is in this world so are we!" But Jesus said we would be provisioned for greater works than He had accomplished. *Christian* means being Christ-like, not mimicking it. Satan also knows the Scripture and trembles. Knowing the truth is not the benchmark of the Christian striving; it's a means to the end—becoming truly Christian. "Then said Jesus to those Jews which believed on him, If ye continue in my word, then are ye my disciples indeed; and ye shall know the truth, and the truth shall make you free" (John 8:31–32 KJV). I have heard these lines misrepresented and applied to so many out-of-context needs. The gospel sets us free, but how does it do that? What's the meaning and manner of the freedom promised through the gospel? These may seem inconsequential questions, but we must find their answers for ourselves and others.

I have seen drunken preachers expound the gospel articulately and vociferously and stir their congregations to their feet in tears; even pedophile clergymen can deliver soul-searching sermons and inspire their congregations to praise the Lord sincerely. In such cases, the liberating truth of the gospel was not in the preachers, but their darkness does not inhibit their listeners' desires.

These kinds of contemplations are extensive throughout the body, although people hardly raise them, and they produce negative effects on many who come into contact with such dysfunctional leadership. I have listened to the Word, I believed the Word, but why am I not free? Why am I developing anxiety and depression about tomorrow? The answer lies deep in this seemingly ambiguous statement. Do the Word.

Do the Word. Be a doer! It's inexcusable and irresponsible to tell children of God to be strong in the Lord without first telling them what strength is and how to develop it. Telling someone to pray and study is good but inadequate; prayer and study can contribute greatly to growth, but there's a danger in suggesting that this advice is an all-inclusive package of Christianity. Prayer and study are key elements of Christian well-being, but they cannot make Christians strong in and of themselves; they themselves need to strengthen continuously.

Nonetheless, we need to develop strong and consistent prayer lives founded in the Scriptures. Just knowing is not enough; we must do the Word. John said, "In the beginning was the word … and the word became flesh"; the flesh must become the Word. By the grace of God, in the following chapters I hope to transform stagnation into growth that will rejuvenate your spiritual desires. Don't labor over the thought of the flesh becoming the Word; the carnal, Adamic nature is called the flesh; the spiritual nature is Christ on the inside.

Christ must dwell in us is a reference to the new man, the new creation that is essentially the mind and nature of the man Christ Jesus. Christ must be formed in us; we must become the fruit of the Spirit according to Galatians. Putting off the old nature and being renewed means developing the characteristics of Christ until He is personified in us. Peter said God was love, so we cannot just hope to practice love if we are striving for godliness in love; we must be love. Just as hate is a spirit, so is love. The Word tells us that as He was in this world, and so are we. We must personify love. We acquired our hate nature at birth as a consequence of our progenitors' fall. When we dethrone hate, we take on love. Rattling off the love

Scriptures is not love. Though we may not know it, love requires us to act as God would until we do so unconsciously. This is called striving to become love; it does not mean we are performing to attract the love of others.

Striving is not Christ like; you may deem that statement harsh, but being is the indication of the nature. Christians have a tendency to say, "I'm not where I should be, but I am not where I used to be." Well, they are on their way, and I encourage them to continue on their Christian growth process.

> For if any be a hearer of the word, and not a doer, he is like unto a man beholding his natural face in a glass: For he beholdeth himself, and goeth his way, and straightway forgetteth what manner of man he was. But whoso looketh into the perfect law of liberty, and continueth therein, he being not a forgetful hearer, but a doer of the work, this man shall be blessed in his deed. (James 1:23–25 KJV)

James said the Word is a mirror. The apostle used this metaphor to show the reality of the Word. What he meant was it duplicated the image of who we were and in it we saw realistic replications of ourselves for who we truly can become. Its instruction is geared to turning us into whom we should be. Unless we do what the Word says, we will have no potential for real growth. Hearing the Word but not doing what it says amounts to soul neglect.

How do we start changing? I'm reluctant to suggest supplemental support apart from the Word; we're advised to develop the mind of Christ: "Let this mind be in you which was also in Christ Jesus. (Phillipians 2:5 KJV)" This Scripture explicitly tells us what the mind of Christ is, but do we know what it is? To find an answer to this question, we will need to research supplemental literature including some from psychiatry. This field of study will teach you how to build your mind. Search Scripture to determine the characteristics of Jesus' mind-set and build on that.

The deceitfulness in this surfaces when we contrive assumptions to sway or even convince ourselves that our solution is sufficient. This is a case of knowingly and willfully defrauding ourselves by entertaining the idea that we have answered the question. Behavior like this results in exposing ourselves as surrogates to a flagrant incapacitation of our souls.

We will use the analogy of the seed and the soul to demonstrate the necessary change. The soil's condition was of the utmost concern to the Lord in the parable, so understanding the role of the seed in this parable is essential to its central message. The soil represents our souls, our psyches. In this parable, we can deduce that it is a reflection on grace, a time of optimum preparedness; otherwise, the sower couldn't be the Lord Jesus Christ.

First, was the wayside seed expected to grow? This is a tough question; because the seed was sown, someone put it there. "For God so loved the world, that he gave his only begotten son, that whosoever believeth in him should not perish but have everlasting life." (John 3:16 KJV) Although we know that not all who encounter the Savior will become productive, we're sure the provisions for growth had been established, so we can't blame the sower.

The stages of preparedness of soil in the parable illustrate the susceptibility of the comers. The field represents the world, and therefore it cannot mean a personal witness. Jesus said, "In the day you hear my voice don't harden your heart."

Last, was life possible under those conditions? The sower sowed the seed with the expectation that it would grow, that we would all have the chance to hear. However, the soil of the wayside lacked the qualities necessary for growth.

Without the death of the seed, a plant will not be born. The death of the seed is essential to its beginning as a unique life. Our Lord said that one of the greater characteristics of the seed is its readiness to die. A silo of grain profits little in comparison to a freshly manicured field planted with seeds that mature. "Verily, verily, I say unto you, except a corn of wheat fall into the ground and die, it abideth alone: but if it die, it bringeth forth much fruit. (John 12:24 KJV)" Considering that, let's give serious consideration to this lesson for a minute. There isn't sufficient evidence to evaluate the death or growth process of the seed from our text. There certainly is a natural process of germination; we expect seeds that fall on good ground will grow and produce life though it will be different from the seed.

We know the seed's needs: water, nourishment from the soil, and photosynthesis; a well-prepared soil contains all these. A new plant must undergo developmental stages before it will produce seeds. First comes the blade, then the flowers, and finally the ear. We plant a seed to yield a harvest in accordance with its nature. We know a seed will not produce seeds but will produce a plant that will produce seeds.

How does this concept apply to the gospel principles of growth and strength? How to become strong is a challenge for many Christians. How does the gospel make us strong and Christ like? I have heard so many devout Christian recite like poets full of conviction Scripture taken from "For **God hath not given us the spirit of fear**; but **of** power, and **of** love, and **of** a sound mind." (2 Timothy 1:7 KJV) So frequently is this quoted that I have dubbed it the power enhancer, but lamentably, I witness these enthusiasts shaking in their boots at the smallest uncertainties. I'm not convinced at all they understood well enough what they were trying to grasp. Even with apparent great and sincere conviction, what they say doesn't match what they do. Their actions march to another drum and are unfortunately more convincing than words.

Actions are indicative of heartfelt desires; lips present only hope. "For **as** he **thinketh in his heart**, so is he!" (Proverbs 23:7 KJV) The word said, "This people **draw**eth **nigh** unto **me with their mouth**, and honoureth **me with their** lips; but **their** heart is far from **me**." (Matthew 15:8 KJV) The heart referred to is the soul, the seat of emotions, desires, and character.

The deeper meaning here spells out the conditions of an unregenerate heart; it cannot draw close to God because it hasn't been illuminated by the Spirit. This is frustrating for those endeavoring to put their best faith foot forward only to have their intentions destabilized by their anticipation. Doubts are fed through sensory perception.

Sensory predispositions obviously diminish good intentions; reality is too idiosyncratic. We cannot rely on our own understanding to be desensitized to the harshness of trials; something more than self is needed. The father who brought his troubled child to Christ raised the same despairing doubt about his inability to go beyond sense. He said, "Lord, I believe; **help** thou mine **unbelief**." (Mark 9:24 KJV) Something in the man knew Jesus was able to answer his need, but something else in him stopped its manifestation. He had all the necessary knowledge, but calling upon this knowledge, he fell tragically into despair. What he knew couldn't produce enough faith. He thought his child was as good as dead though he knew he was standing in the presence of the life giver. What is it that convinces us we cannot succeed in situations in which so many others have succeeded?

This lesson teaches us we need more knowledge than this man had. There has to be more than what accompanied this man. He knew what to believe and on whom to center that belief, but when the test of his faith arrived, he found out his knowledge was inadequate.

I am persuaded that being Christ like is much more than just beautiful presentations and reciting the Word. It must amount to more than just saying the word; If Christlikeness is not cultivated in us, the result will be bewilderment and we will abandon our hopes and dreams. This is when many good-intentioned Christians have walked out of church doors vowing never to return. They had assumed they were good Christians but for some unperceived reason had concluded God didn't care about their efforts when in reality it wasn't God at all.

My dear friend, this is a dilemma we face; there's no stopping churches' revolving doors. We must learn how to change directions to grow. Scripture gives us many hints about how to do this. Paul suggested that living in Christ was the ideal mentality for nurturing strength: "Let the word of Christ dwell in you richly in all wisdom; teaching and admonishing one another in psalms and hymns and spiritual songs, singing with grace in your hearts to the Lord." (Colossians 3:16 KJV)

At conversion, believers receive the nature of Christ embryonically. Thereafter, they have two natures, the old and the new, and they are at war with each other. The flesh wars against the Spirit and the Spirit against the flesh from the onset. The apostle believed the nature of the evolving characters would eventually destroy the deeds of the flesh. He warned his readers to crucify the deeds of the body. That will take time mainly because it involves mental changes. Nothing sustainable will be experienced until our desire is in subjection. This will certainly aid the Spirit by reducing the ability of the flesh to contend with it. However, the precise course of action to enforce these great teachings is convoluted.

There are no clear directions on how to appropriate strength from the gospel, so difficulties persist in how to answer the question, how does the gospel make us strong? We could reach a consensus on the answer if we had Paul's mind-set: "But be ye doers of the word, and not hearers only, deceiving your own selves. For if any be a hearer of the word, and not a doer, he is like unto a man beholding his natural face in a glass." (James 1:22-23 KJV) This will serve as an equitable introduction, or a paradigm of some sort, on how to strengthen one-self. In this lesson there is a method of approach that offers an idea to at least a theoretical point of view, to what is Christian strength, and how it is cultivated. We must become doers, not just hearers of the Word: "Don't just become hearers, but become doers of the word." How to do the gospel seems very much to be connected to what is missing for many of us; until we learn how to do the gospel, we won't be able to be the gospel. In other words, light is not lips service it is character projection. The Beatitudes in Matthew's gospel have a number of paradigms we will explore as possible sources of direction.

The Word of God offers a clear path to Christian living, especially the doctrines of the Lord Jesus Christ and the apostles, but we will identify the truth only by the Holy Spirit's direction. This is spiritual awakening through the Spirit. Even Satan is very familiar with the Scripture and can quote it for his purposes, but just quoting Scripture means little; doing Scripture is what counts. That leads to. Doing what the word instructs us is the beginning path to spiritual growth. Practicing will certainly facilitate growth. In his letter to the Philippians, Paul wrote,

But made himself of no reputation, and took upon him the form of a servant, and was made in the likeness of men: And being found in fashion as a man, he humbled himself, and became obedient unto death, even the death of the cross. (Philippians 2:7 KJV)

Our Lord Jesus Christ came from the bosom the Father, wrapped Himself in the garment of flesh, and assumed the duties of a slave. We will return to this subject later in much greater detail, but for now, we must understand what the apostle meant. There are scores of teaching on where, with whom, and how Jesus received his education: "And the child grew, and waxed strong in spirit, filled with wisdom and the grace of God was upon him ... And Jesus increased in wisdom and stature, and in favor with God and man" (Luke 2:40, 52 KJV).

Let us go back to the pre-incarnate position of the Son, to begin our inquiry into this lesson. The introduction to John's gospel gives clear insight into role of the pre-incarnate Son. John aligned the introduction of his gospel to that of the Book of Genesis, and this is no coincidence. The apostle purposefully began his work this way to draw on the parallel information presented in the two beginnings. He wrote, "In the beginning was the Word and the Word was with God, and the Word was God." (John 1:1 KJV) ". . . and the Word became flesh..." (John 1:14 KJV)

John wrote his gospel in Greek because it was the national language spoken by the Roman Empire. Aramaic was the local language spoken by the Jews. To understand John's intention, in introduction of the Son, we must understand John's use of the Greek word *logos*, "word," which also denotes "wisdom," "reasoning," "affection" and "desire." "In the beginning was the Word," The etymological Greek root for word is Logos "Word." In its Greek root form this word means much more than just spoken language. It denotes: Words, Wisdom, Reasoning, Affection and Desire. The apostle said that the Word became flesh. Jesus is the psyche of God, the intellect of God. This qualifies Jesus to be the light and life of God.

He is the creative force in the Trinity. When God breathed, *pneuma*, He breathed into Christ the Word, the wisdom, the reasoning, the affection, and the desire of God. His attributes are spiritual in nature. We believers must mortify our sensual spirit nature and seek to cultivate in us His Spirit nature.

Raising this point on Paul's writing to the Philippians gathers a number of essential components of this lesson. The Word became flesh to redeem those who were under the law and bring them into son-ship with God. But one great truth here is that this was not the simple act of role reversal or role-playing. First, the apostle described him as the Son who became the Son of man. This act is just as realistic as the slaves becoming sons. Last, He became sin so we might become righteous. For this reason, we can grow up in Him in all things. But being simply content with knowing these great teachings is self-defeating. We have the capacity to become, but we will capitalize on that only by implementing any changes intrinsically until we are one in Him.

You perhaps have heard about the deep, dark, empty void in all hearts even after salvation has come; this is the spiritual connection of which we now speak. We cannot experience peace in our hearts until we become peace, nor will we be loved until we become love. God replenishes these qualities in us, His latent children. We must cultivate these characteristics and build on them to achieve Christ's maturity and perfection.

Our bodies are the temple of the living God. At conversion, He takes up residence in our hearts, and that begins our shift from our old, Adamic nature.

Through Christ, we leave behind our fallen nature and take on God's characteristics. These divine natures are the fruit of the Spirit—love, joy, peace, longsuffering, gentleness, goodness, faith, meekness, and temperance. When they replace what we were born with, God is being formed in our hearts.

Strength doesn't come from hearing but from doing and becoming. Have you ever wondered what is meant by, "God is a spirit and they that worship him must worship him in spirit and in truth"? (John 4:24 KJV) Understanding this begins with knowing that God is a Spirit, and to worship Him, the worshiper must be spirit. It is not by might nor by power but by my Spirit, said the Lord. To worship requires worshiping in spirit and in truth, the fruit of the Spirit. I'm aware of the emotional frenzies considered worship. God is love, so love must be a spirit. So then we agree that hate, the opposite of love, is also a spirit.

The collection of information gathered by the senses is not solely fleshly. Even psychiatrists, the experts in the field of Psychiatry aren't sure how they affect us spiritually and physically. I'm no psychiatrist, but I know this information finds its way into our thinking and affects us incredibly, even altering our senses, this information's source. They must be spirits. This means we can become like Christ, and I daresay this isn't an arduous task.

The mind operates in the spirit as well as in the flesh and blood. If we accept the spirit help we are given and turn our thoughts from the world, the sensual seems very much accomplishable. The Bible said, "Love not the world neither the things in the world." (1 John 2:15 KJV) These are the sources of sensual inspiration. When these sensations or stimulations enter us through our senses, a spirit of change is introduced first, and then they enter and rest in the mind. No matter the nature of the sensory stimulation, it will alter us and effect changes. If those sensations are desirable, the mind is transformed and our characters shift accordingly.

Character changes produce habit-forming behavior. When impatience becomes meekness, a trait of the Spirit is born; we become Christ like in our hearts and Christ resides there. It is becoming no longer I who live, but Christ who lives in me. What then is Christ in us? Longsuffering, peace, and gentleness that incubate in our spirits is the formation of Christ by faith. These godlike characteristics we cultivate are the gifted and attainable elements of His divine nature.

The acquisition of such is the beginning of a life in Christ in us, the hope of glory. Have you ever wondered why the apostle wrote at the end of the presentation of the fruit of the Spirit, "Against such there is no law"? Well, all these new, pure, spiritual characteristics are guiding principles and are the attributes of God. Meekness, gentleness, and patience cause a spiritual awakening and strengthening because they are the characteristics of our godliness and will potentially mature us in our likeness of Him. They are what Christ came to bestow. He called them mature fruits in Luke 8. Keep in mind they are more paradigms than lessons. It is here that we seek this perfection.

Jesus is the Logos, the psyche of God, Christ's essence. Jesus said, "I am the vine, ye are the branches: He that abideth in me, and I in him, the same bringeth forth much fruit: for without me ye can do nothing." (John 15:5 KJV) Another way to look at this analogy is through the paralleling used by the Lord. The great characteristic of Christ has been transferred to us through the discipline of the vine. This is the essential divine nature we are being transformed into; the sap flows from the vine to the branch. It's not conferred upon us; we grow up in Him. This great stretch of imagination is called the oneness principle.

We must not negate the prerequisite of works that accompany changes. There are no ready-made changes; they come about through conversion by faith and work, through the commitment to persevere in spite of trials and errors. If we are serious about being more than just mere speakers of the Word, we must work to be transformed into and nourish the qualities that come from the Father through the Son which were manifested out from the bosom of the Father through the Son of man.

> Let the word of Christ dwell in you richly in all wisdom; teaching and admonishing one another in psalms and hymns and spiritual songs, singing with grace in your hearts to the Lord. (Colossians 3:16 KJV)

The Lord taught us to dwell in Him: "Abide in me, and I in you. As the branch cannot bear fruit of itself, except it abide in the vine; no more can ye, except ye abide in me." (John 15:4 KJV) Abiding in Christ means accepting His Word and doctrines, marks of discipleship.

Adherence to the truths of the word is a mark of discipleship. This abiding reaches permanency when it is allowed to mature; by this progression, the Word becomes character. When such growth is confirmed, it produces permanence. By being allowed to take root, it produces deep-seated roots, will produce in us a resemblance of Him, further mature, and produce power and authority in our lives.

When we develop a true and enthusiastic reverence for the Word and venerate it above our human necessities we grow spiritually, it is a clear indication of growth. When we hold fast to the aptitude of the word consistently and, with consistency and enthusiastically and follow scriptural direction, we are striving for maturity. This is evidence of the solemnity of the promise that we "shall continue in the Son and in the Father." The blessings and privileges we will enjoy are the glory of the oneness, the same spirit, the same love, the same miraculous power operating in us. In John 14:12 (KJV), we read, "Verily, verily, I say unto you, He that believeth on me, the works that I do shall he do also; and greater works than these shall he do; because I go unto my Father!"

We must constantly remind ourselves that our bodies are the temples of the living God and the fruit of the Spirit and that God's characteristics have replaced the spirit of the flesh and are His nature at work in us. "Christ in me the Hope of glory."

Here is an enthusiastic thought that goes well with the teaching that the meek shall inherit the earth. The earth is the Lord's, and through becoming meek like God, He can empower us to operate in exclusivity in our newly acquired dominion capacity of inheritance. When we become like a thing, we have its intrinsic qualities. This compel us to act, think, and seek to feel like the mentor we want to become. As He is in this world, so are we.

Chapter 1

Salvation

We have already touched on the subject of salvation in the introduction, but since salvation is a theme of this work, let us define it. This chapter will deal with the purpose and procedure of salvation.

Almost immediately after the fall, our Creator implemented a process whereby we could reunite with Him. His plan of salvation incorporates many complex concepts that while simple in terms of operation, their structure is complex, and their developmental structures pose huge perplexities. In these multifarious perceptions connected by subtle tones and meanings of interconnectedness, we will find their understanding to be indescribable. Many of the tones and meanings we encounter are inferential and at best can be thought of only as opinions.

The Bible clearly teaches that the plan of salvation was a foreordained purpose conceived in the mind of the Ancient of Days. While we know what the word *salvation* means, sectarian dogmas will arise, challenge our purpose, and create many conflicts.

It is interesting to note that the local vernacular of the Hebrew, Greek, and Latin diaspora share similarities regarding the definition of *salvation*. The Greek word *soteria*, the Latin word *salvatio*, and the Hebrew word *yeshu'ah* all suggest almost the same definition: being saved or protected from harm or delivered from some dire consequence. But this definition doesn't express the essence of the word. Because the plan of salvation was implemented as a consequence of sin, the word *salvation* refers more to the concerns of a present and eternal spiritual restoration of the soul.

God did not just intend to deliver us from sin; His purpose was much grander. His plan included reinstating and repositioning humanity into the economy and government with authority. Salvation includes not only the forgiveness of sin but also the reestablishment of humanity's authority and ability. It's significantly more than a simple search-and-rescue mission.

When we are born again, we are born into the family of God; His likeness and image are restored in us. Those who are born again receive power to become the children of God. In this context, the idea of *power* refers to a broad platform of authorities and abilities.

Sin must always be regarded as spiritual cancer that salvation cures. Some folks are in hunches and bunches over the possibility of acquiring wealth, but to know God in the intimacy of a father-and-son relationship is the endearing lure.

Sin has created a void in us that drives us to medicate our minds. The gorge in our soul gapes because of the absence of fellowship with our Maker. Jesus came that we might have life—and life more abundantly. Understanding this promise is necessary for our understanding of salvation. The Lord gave up His life for our sins so that we might be born again. He is the light that will light the lamp of God. Salvation is the plan that will prepare us, deliver us, and restore us. Hallelujah!

Dispensations

I'm well aware of the dispensational overtones in this book, but while we see and agree with the divisions called dispensations, we don't support the idea that dispensations are terminating.

I don't dogmatically propose that these periods be recognized and renamed "cycles" just to create a new dogma. I want only that you become aware of these eras as specific interventions set up in the plan of salvation. Most significantly, they continue and will culminate in the fullness of time. Their nature and purpose will unfold as we move further into our studies.

Eden and the Fall

The controlled environment in Eden was an incubator, a nursery. Jehovah blessed everything He had created—except the firmament; that shouldn't go unnoticed. The dark, submerged world seems to have been the punishment for those who occupied the pre-Edenic world for some reason we don't know. However, as a consequence, we know that somewhere and by some means, our progenitors, earth's new population, would have engaged the spirits of the firmament.

This idea is only speculative, but because the firmament wasn't blessed in the creation process, we assume it was the abode of a fallen race. It would be highly conceivable that those inhabitants would eventually have engaged our forebears.

4

With that thought in mind, let us consider the latency in which our predecessors begun. It is very much conceivable to imagine that Eden could have been a preparatory estuary, a place of security and protection that were essential then; it was. We may define the nature of Eden as a nurturing environment. We must not be shortsighted about the eminently dangerous atmosphere of the place.

Things set up for maturity could be devastating for innocence. The Tree of the Knowledge of Good and Evil, for example, seems to have been an extremely forceful magnet to the neighbors; this is clearly understood from the instruction by Jehovah that any interaction with the tree would result in death. But the Tree of the Knowledge of Good and Evil tree was not the only danger in Eden; elsewhere in the garden was the Tree of Life.

God placed these trees in Eden for the benefit of humanity at a later stage in its maturity, but because of the catastrophic nature of the fall, the maturity process that would have prepared humanity for this higher-order consumption was marred. For humanity's good, Jehovah shut down Eden and invigorated the plan of salvation, an extended preparatory epoch.

Prior to the fall, humanity knew only one sin, one way to transgress the will of its Creator. We must dismiss any ignorance that obscures our attention to the Tree of the Knowledge of Good and Evil. Eating the fruits of all the other trees in the garden was permissible; by contrast, this unshielded, accessible, and extremely tantalizing tree bore exceedingly poisonous fruit. Humanity needed maturity to handle these spiritual uncertainties. The cycles are God's timeframe for the development of these provisions.

Restoration

Salvation's ultimate purpose is a plan of restoration. All the cycles contained faith and grace, and all the provisional elements for developing maturity are perpetuated developmentally until they reach their completion in the fullness of time (see chapter 11, "Maturity and the Perfect Man"). All will come to a climax when the Father places everything in heaven and on earth under the control of the man Christ Jesus. This will bring to manifestation the saying by the prophet Isaiah, "Unto us a child is born, unto us a Son is given and the Government would be upon his shoulder." The Father will make our Lord (who is every whit God and every whit man) the head of the only true theocratic government.

When the perfect man reigns, salvation's restoration will be completed. The Lord Jesus Christ released this information on the Mount of Transfiguration. He told His disciples that all the powers in heaven and earth were already under His jurisdiction, that shortly thereafter He would return dominion to humanity, and that whatever they bound on earth would be bound in heaven and whatever they loosed on earth would be loosed in heaven. Earth awaits its fiery renovation restoration.

Chapter 2

The Bible

One evening, I was flipping through the hundreds of TV channels and stumbled upon a stand-up comedy special. The comedian was a middle-aged Jewish comedian. He was well into his act, spouting off about "his" book, the Jewish Bible. The comedy was a seriously jaded satire on the religiosity and cultural intolerance of one religion against another religion, particularly by unqualified Christian zealots.

Among the comedian's many topics was a burlesque caricature of televangelist gospel preachers. He ridiculed these preachers for having the audacity to want their own Bible because, according to him, the Old Testament was no longer good enough for them. It was too old, so they needed a new Bible. He said

The main point of his routine was the idea that on their Lord's Day, gospel preachers preached to the church out of his book—the Old Testament. He said that though they claimed they needed a new book, they were too ill-equipped and ill-informed to interpret the old book. This guy suggested that rather than say dumb, ignorant things, they should get someone qualified to interpret it for them since the Old Testament was the book of another culture.

From a general perspective, this comedian shed credible light of the nature of our inquiry. First, Christian scholars, not Jewish scholars, introduced the idea of an Old Testament. The Jews believe that the Abrahamic and Sinaic covenants are still emerging and active. They believe these covenants are still activated. They are eagerly anticipating the Messiah, the protagonist of the new book.

Is there any truth to their belief? Yes! Nothing Jehovah has implemented on behalf of spiritual maturity has ended. There is neither any vital need nor any plausible explanation for so crudely dividing the Bible into old and new compartments.

To understand the development of the concept of the Old and New Testaments, we must adhere to the strictest conformity to scholarly interpretation if we want to have any hope of gaining benefit or understanding from this study. A comprehensive approach must begin with this very rhetorical but fundamentally significant question: is there a real distinction between the New and the Old Testament? Discovering what constituted our Bible would be of benefit to us. What knowledge do we have about the structure of the Bible, and what if any imposing evidence exists to validate grounds for an Old and a New Testament? These are the principal concepts of our inquiries this chapter will address.

We must regard this inquiry as a critical step because some see great discrepancies in the progressive structure of biblical formats; any deviation or rejection must be clearly understood and explained or the plan of salvation might be seen as an unimportant human construct. These variations have become extremely disruptive to the continuity of the flow of salvation's developmental increments, thus creating powerful but unsubstantiated dogmas.

Although I may seem to be courting the theory of dispensationalism, I am not. Though there are no necessary grounds to reject the dispensationalist presentiments, I am not defending or rejecting its dogma.

There are many schools of thought on salvation, and they are separated by very great theoretical ideas about the purpose and intent of the Bible's structure. The dispensationalists consider dispensations as divinely appointed administrative periods ordained by

Jehovah to order the affairs of the world. Many of their theories developed through the covenants God made with humanity. Our only difference in theory is that there are conscientious and cumulative principles in each of the cycles God requires us to grasp; these will mature in time.

> For where a testament is, there must also of necessity be the death of the testator. For a testament is of force after men are dead: otherwise it is of no strength at all while the testator liveth. Whereupon neither the first testament was dedicated without blood. For when Moses had spoken every precept to all the people according to the law, he took the blood of calves and of goats, with water, and scarlet wool, and hyssop, and sprinkled both the book, and all the people, Saying, This is the blood of the testament which God hath enjoined unto you. (Hebrews 9:16–20 KJV)

The modern Bible is composed of two Testaments, an Old and a New. Our major struggle is with determining whether there is legitimate ground to substantiate the validity of two testaments or even seven for that matter. Apart from the radical extremist dogmas, the uncertainty of this answer is entangled in the definition of the word *testament*, the word testament is derived from the Latin word '*testamentum* In the Law and the prophets, the Hebrew form of the word is *b'rit*. The Greek word for *testament* is *diatheke.* A problem arises with diatheke; it also means. The word *diatheke* also means "covenant," but. It is very interesting to discover that the Hebrew b'rit, testamentum, and diatheke have a general sense of agreement in their definitions of the word *testament*. When we understand that the words *covenant* and *testament* are used interchangeably throughout Scripture, and most scholars agree, that can eliminate a huge number of discrepancies.

The modern interpretation of the etymological roots of both words' definitions may reveal some subtleties in their differences. This bit of information, though subtle, warrants investigation. We have already discovered that many scholars adhere to the thought that there is an inherent interchangeability in the meaning of covenant and testament, however, knowing the subtleties of difference is critical to our ability to understand the usage of this application and the enforcement of these words.

A covenant is an arbitrary agreement, a contract written or otherwise between two people that is binding as long as both parties are alive and willing to enforce it. Upon the death of any of the parties, the covenant becomes null and void and all arbitrary stipulations are terminated. At the moment, it is only necessary to say here that there are seven general covenants in the Bible. It will not be necessary to go into the details of the seven general covenants in the Bible because information on them is readily available and they have been discussed by many translators. All through biblical history, God has been making these agreements, or covenants with man, for whatever his divine prerogatives may have determined; they were. The concept of a covenant is an agreement by which God and humanity worked to enforce and extend a principle.

A testamentary trust is a legal arrangement created by a testator and goes into effect only upon the testator's death. It is not effective until the testator is deceased. There are biblical grounds for distinguishing between covenants and testaments: "For where a testament is, there must also of necessity be the death of the testator. For a testament is of force after men are dead: otherwise it is of no strength at all while the testator liveth" (Hebrews 9:16–17 KJV).

A testament is not contractual and is not contingent upon mutual agreement. A standard definition of a testament is a will, a testamentary trust. Noting the differences between what he calls the Old and New Testament, the apostle Paul made a huge effort to differentiate between a covenant and a testament but didn't elaborate on the differences. He seemed to use covenant and testament interchangeably.

> For when Moses had spoken every precept to all the people according to the law, he took the blood of calves and of goats, with water, and scarlet wool, and hyssop, and sprinkled both the book, and all the people, Saying, This is the blood of the testament which God hath enjoined unto you. Moreover he sprinkled with blood both the tabernacle, and all the vessels of the ministry. (Hebrews 9:19–22 KJV)

We see clearly what Paul alluded to in verses 19–21 (KJV) when he called the Sinaic covenant a testament; Moses did use blood to bind the covenant.

But that's not what he actually wrote in verse 16: "For where a testament is, there must also of necessity be the death of the testator." Calves and goats are not testators; they cannot be. A Testator is the person who write wills. Borrowing from his discourses on the law, we see that he used calves and goats as types of Christ, and there is no reason why we should amend this. He had already stated that the blood of bulls and goats couldn't produce perfection, so there is no reason why we should not understand the apostle to mean that verses 19–21 are symbolic of the true testament that had been established through the body and blood of the Lord Jesus Christ.

Prior to grace, we have had five such covenants, all of which have come under the banner of the Old Testament. This may be trivial. They were all ratified by blood, so we could argue that. Making a valid case that according to the disputed definition, we have had six testaments. We can now agree that they are covenants primarily because of their ceremonial presentation and the fact that they are congruous in the fundamentals of faith, obedience, and grace though the ruling factor that their developmental stages differ. These principles are the ruling pedagogues presented as the major ruling principle in each cycle.

A major point of reference is being developed here, is there a legitimate difference between the Old and New Testaments? If so, is there central, focal information that distinguishes one from the other? If so, what is the central source of information that legitimizes the Old Testament as a testament? Let us keep in mind the criteria put forth in Hebrews 9, according to which only one testament fit this prototype—the testimony about the work of the Lord Jesus Christ. He was the only person throughout Scriptures who died to validate a will. Moses was not a testator.

The Bible is fundamentally a compilation of dispensational cycles segmented by covenants and other divine events. These cycles are structured through the contractual arrangements or covenants. The gist of this point of view is relatively simple: do the contractual elements and the covenants ever terminate or are they continuous?

All Scriptural movement seems to point to continuous and indefinite developmental progression flowing indefinitely as is seen in the structures of the covenants or contracts in dispensational or developmental cycles. This we all can agree upon to some extent.

Major disagreements have surfaced with the idea that the developmental cycles and their covenants are regarded by many as separate, unique events that terminate in the era; they are treated as means to ends. There is no evidence that anything Jehovah began in Genesis has reached completion outside of the Lord Jesus Christ, so we must never see this as likely.

Bunching these developmental cycles into two groups to form either an Old or New Testament is not founded or biblically supported. From the day Jehovah said to the Devil, "His heel will bruise your head," the process of obtaining that manifestation continued until the Messiah, the manifestation of the seed. He implemented this plan through the presentation of types and antitypes until its fulfillment in the cycle of grace.

Many Bible scholars and students treat the life of Jesus as insignificant in terms of its biblical placement, but it is significant if we are to focus on such philosophies as Old and New Testaments. The place and purpose of the life and times of the Messiah in Scripture is fundamentally significant; it has great implications for the era of maturity and the division of the Bible.

First, it must be acknowledged that Christ the Messiah came under the cycle of the Law and all His works prior to His death transpired under the law, under strict conformity with to the Levitical ordinances.

The Lord grew up a devout Jew and a prominent worshiper in the synagogues. Many people misunderstood His strict conformity to the law for a number of reasons, mainly because of His staunch criticism of and opposition to it. He berated the scribes and leaders for following the traditional rule of interpreting the Scriptures. Many Bible teachers labor under extreme shortsightedness in understanding the place of the Lord in Scripture because of the way He berated the leaders' preposterous reverence for Jewish traditions, but as a Jew, He followed the Law to the letter.

What authority is there to place Jesus' life and times in the New Testament? He lived and died an orthodox Jew under strict conformity to the Law. If His resurrection ushered in the cycle of grace, neither His miracles nor His teachings happened in that cycle. The gospel writer wrote, "He came unto **his own**, and **his own received him not.**" (John 1:11 KJV) It would seem that only the rejection of Jesus' person and work and the bitter hatred they gave rose to catapult Him into the so-called New Testament. The truth is simple and clear: He had to live a Jewish life and die a Jewish death under the absolute jurisdiction of the law.

His resurrection and ascension in the cycle of grace removed any association He had with the first Adam.

He was called the Seed of Abraham. But Jehovah forged a seamless connection to the beginning of the salvation plan He had implemented in Eden. Jesus' life and times were amalgamated; there is no dichotomy. No provisions exist for Him to be either a New or an Old Testament subject; He was the completion of the plan of salvation.

To add to this obvious erroneous misinterpretation of Scripture, some biblical interpreters dare to see a different contingency in the plan of redemption. They blame the double-mindedness of Jehovah, who according to their doctrines alleged that God was practically and functionally different in His providential activities with humanity in the two unique time periods.

In the Old Testament, He was described as imperiously ill-tempered and rancorous. He was reactive in the Old, exacting extraneous punishments seemingly temperamentally on anyone who fell short of His will. However, they insist that in the New Testament, He was proactive, patient, longsuffering, and mild mannered with the gospel saints, even asking that they call Him Father, whereas in the Old Testament, anyone who dared approach Him was immediately consumed. He demanded strict reverence to His name.

Those who hold these preposterous notions say that one of the most compelling distinguishing features of the two testaments is the clear differences in Jehovah's responsive actions and interactions in the two Testament periods. The repulsiveness of this idea is invigorated through the ridiculous claim that "The God of the Old Testament was a God of wrath, whereas the God of the New Testament tempered His providence in love. He portrayed Himself as loveable."

God was and still is a God of love. I've even heard suggestions that the actions and interactions of God in the New Testament could be compared to that of a grandmother. He treated the church saints as His grandchildren, whereas He treated the Old Testament saints were treated like His children. You can see just how devious these insinuations are; the idea would be more meaningful if you had ever experienced such treatment as a child. My mom forbade us to enter any part of the living room, but now you see your children eating and playing there under the encouraging eyes and delight of their granny. The Lord bids us come boldly and as often as we desire, whereas Israel was invited once a year, and that entailed great pomp and circumstance.

I cannot agree with the tone of this statement or its point of view, but in my day, had I dared to dream of eating in my mother's living room, I would have had to have donned sackcloth and ashes. Jehovah was becoming soft, they say! What do I say? Preposterous! Jehovah declared, "I am the Lord and I do not change."

Sure, Israel was punished for its recalcitrance, but let's not forget His provisions of mercy and protection; His patience and longsuffering were equally facilitated in every act of their disobedience. The church is being punished in the same manner for its disobedience just as Israel had been punished for its stubbornness.

If we are to convey a message of hope, we must not contrive dogmatism to bolster our independent notions. No Scripture should be privately interpreted, and anyone who wishes to create sacred rites or bend Scriptures to fit an agenda is acting outside God's will. We must not seek to have our ideologies putative through unscrupulous findings and shortsightedness of the truth. True, some are so eager to be different that they go to extremes to sound provocative even to the extent of compromising the Scriptures' purpose.

The judges and the prophets were messengers of God's mercies; they were the bearers of general and personal messages from Jehovah that called for compliance and repentance regardless of stations in life. The book of Hosea is an archival paradigm of

God's care and patience in the face of Israel's blatant, continuous noncompliance, but even so, Jehovah said He was married to the transgressor. This message was dramatically presented through the actions and reactions of Hosea and Gomer to each other. God used this prophet to demonstrate to Israel that He had committed to His Word.

The insinuation that the church is treated like His grandchildren is preposterous; those who foster that view are shortsighted. The Bible is the history of the revelation of God's development of humanity; it shows the unfolding of God's character and personality as humanity matures. This process should be more obvious as humanity becomes more spiritually and mentally mature. His omniscience can be revealed as the developmental cycle matures. This is brought out through the available reference to theophany and types. We can say that the process increased incrementally from theophany to the manifestation of Jesus Christ.

The Lord Jesus Christ is seated at the right hand of the Father and continually intercedes for the saints. He is in charge of the government and the spiritual economy of the church. Grace also means what the Father is free to do on our behalf after Christ rose from the dead.

God is a Spirit, and His interactions with us are spiritual. The vine produces the sap, and the branch produces the flower and the fruit. The more we spiritually mature, the more God is revealed to us not only through revelation but also through that spiritual maturity. As the image and likeness of God take shape in us, God becomes more and more a reality in our consciousness and our actions are transformed more and more into His.

To bring maturity to fruition, pretests and posttests are necessary to monitor and adjust growth. Job said, "But he knoweth the way that I take: when he hath tried me, I shall come forth as gold." (Job 23:10 KJV) Trial is an unavoidable part of the maturation process.

Gold is "tried," purified, in the smelting process. Prior to his horrific ordeals, Job knew of God only from the traditions of his people's elders; nevertheless, he was mightily rewarded for his piety. He and his goods were vulnerable. Because his claim to ownership of his possessions could be challenged, God had to bring Job to a personal knowledge and understanding of who He was to accomplish the task of legitimizing Job and his possessions. Job had to endure harsh trials because his knowledge of God was not mature. Oftentimes on account of his sons' behavior, he was led to second-guess his confidence in his relationship with God. After an unsubstantiated amount of time, amid mournful laments, Job came to the knowledge that God was purging him.

Trial is a part of the soul's purification process. In Hebrews, God warned against resistance to His trials: "But if ye be without chastisement, whereof all are partakers, then are ye **bastards, and not sons**" (Hebrews 12:8 KJV). This statement refers to the teaching that by the Spirit we receive the adoption of sons and daughters and are to call Jehovah, *Abba*, Father.

It is very evident in the Bible that God is immutable in His nature and person and in the ways He revealed Himself to us; the relationship humanity has had with Him developed; He did not. By any assumed shift in His character, He was only demystifying or manifesting more of His holy personage. He is not changing; He has been revealing Himself in this same way from the covenant of works to the covenant of grace, and we will eventually see him face to face. He cannot reveal himself in any other way than holy and righteous; but as we grow in wisdom, consciousness, and character, we commune more intimately with Him through His spiritual developmental likeness.

We learn that God is Spirit and that He changes in character and deed to create spiritual intimacies. The more we become like Him, the more His intimacies are exposed to us. In times past, God winked because our conscience was latent, but since the manifestation of the Lord Jesus Christ, God has demanded we repent and turn from wicked ways.

The unfaltering love of God is unmistakably proactive in every covenant and in every cycle in the Bible; as well, the disobedient will experience His wrath: "And the times of this ignorance God winked at; but now commandeth all men everywhere to repent" (Acts 17:30 KJV).

If this is an indication of God's dealings with us, it would indicate a swift and punitive retributive system in the cycle of grace. And this attitude wouldn't be the result of an arbitrary or intolerant nature. During the early stages of humanity's development, it could hardly be expected that humanity would act as responsibly and as maturely as it would in the course of grace. Though it was developing conscientiously (and indeed some measured up to the mark of maturity), humanity hadn't yet received holistic spiritual development. But in the cycle of grace, when all was fully prepared and people were able to wait rationally with eager anticipation for the arrival of the Messiah, they were capable of being born anew.

> And the times of this ignorance God winked at; but now commandeth all men everywhere to repent: Because he hath appointed a day, in the which he will judge the world in righteousness by that man whom he hath ordained; whereof he hath given assurance unto all men, in that he hath raised him from the dead. (Acts 17:30 KJV)

Grace is the transition from the hopeless encumbrance of sin. This cycle is the end of the probationary period of immaturity. If God would seem to be more punitive in grace, it would be because a way had been opened up and the call of encouragement had been extended. Consequently, ignorance is not a theme in grace. Salvation's path was now ready for God's Messiah to emerge. Grace is the cycle of the fullness of time.

One of the first subjects we must look closely at in the Bible is its division into sixty-six books.

Chapter 3

In His Likeness and Image

> And God said, Let us make man in our image, after our likeness: and let them have dominion over the fish of the sea, and over the fowl of the air, and over the cattle, and over all the earth, and over every creeping thing that creepeth upon the earth.
> So God created man in his own image, in the image of God created he him; male and female created he them. (Genesis 1:26–27 KJV)

The Christian journey is not a journey of reparation but stages of incremental development on a pilgrimage to maturation. In every development cycle, God intends to add to our mental and spiritual development as we evolve into His divine destiny. The cycles are eras during which God implements processes to rehabilitate and connect with us and draw us closer to Him.

During these distinct epochs, God chaperoned specific aspects of our maturation and development. God does not want to simply rescue us: He wants to sanctify us and give us the knowledge we need to comprehend and become like His Redeemer.

Our maturation was vandalized during the fall; an embryonic humanity was driven from Eden and was seriously unprepared for the task of subduing and managing the earth. The fall proved devastating in significant ways; the worst was the severing of avenues of communication between God and humanity. Also very destructive was the ruin of the purposeful design of Eden.

When we say the fall of humanity, we mean the ramifications we incurred by being insubordinate to God. The first man was terrestrial with heavenly characters and with many latent but great possibilities. He was the only terrestrial being with sovereignty, having been made in the likeness and image of God. He was identical to his heavenly Creator insofar as likeness and image go. Though his true characteristics were embryonic and dormant, he was the perfect man.

And God said, Let us make man in our
image, after our likeness: and let them
have dominion over the fish of the sea,
and over the fowl of the air, and over the
cattle, and over all the earth, and over
every creeping thing that creepeth upon
the earth. (Genesis 1:26 KJV)

What do *image* and *likeness* mean in this context?
We must understand four concepts before we can say.
To begin with, the creation of humanity was recorded
with special reference to its higher nature by and
through what it could communicate to Jehovah and its
ability to exercise dominion over the inferior creation.
Humanity is an amalgamated compound of matter and
latent mental abilities.

Second, God created humanity in his image and
likeness in contrast to the way He formed the rest
of creation, a joint venture of the Trinity as we can
deduce from the phrase "Let us."

Third, we must understand humanity's latent
Edenic constitution; we were created infants whose
constitution was proportionate to the image of the
Creator.

Fourth, we must determine Eden's purpose. Was it an exotic garden God created for humanity to live in forever, or was it meant to be an incubator for a period of gestation? How practical was the time spent? Was the fall a tragedy or the end of humanity's gestation period?

"Let us make man in our image, in our likeness." Understanding this statement is a huge step in the direction of learning the connection and purpose between heaven and earth for humanity. This was seemingly the final enterprise in the course of Creation; the fall destroyed the relationship between God and humanity, so the final consignment of the creation process wouldn't reach maturity until Christ's resurrection. The man and woman were covered with skins in Eden; they were in latency. They would be indwelled again by the creative force of the Spirit only at Pentecost.

"Then the Lord God formed a man from the dust of the ground and breathed into his nostrils the breath of life, and the man became a living being" (Genesis 2:7 KJV). The creative process distinguishes humanity from primates and defines it as more kindred to its Maker through its identity with the image and likeness of God, though we recognize that humanity's fullest potentials were unrealized back then.

Sounds blasphemous? Well, we must realize this without trepidation if we want to fully realize the plan God has for us. This supposition is an important pretext to our ultimate perfection. Consternations are exactly what the enemy would have us feel. God said it first and that settles it! We aren't seeking to establish comparative similarities by trying to identify with the words *image* and *likeness*. God said He created us in His image and after His likeness. Jehovah stands alone as the infinite and incomprehensible God; any notion of our equality with Him should come only as we seek to be more like Him.

We must find out God's intention for us. No study of the likeness of God could possibly be authoritative. *Likeness* and *image* are not intended to define God absolutely, for He is omniscient and omnipotent; the words are meant to define our character in relation to His. We are earthly beings and God is a heavenly being; there can be no complete comparison because even our perfect humanness is yet in many aspects latent and still developing. We can mature only through our Savior and our obedience to Him. He said, "If my word abide in you and you abide in my word, I will abide with you and we will be one." Don't be panicky in the search for your God-oriented constitution; this knowledge will distinguish the hearers of the Word from the doers of the Word. We must uncover our potential to develop a likeness to God before we can turn our embryonic latencies into possibilities for fruition. Through the gospel, we know one day we will sit with Him and Christ, but until then, all creation can only anticipate that.

We cannot think of the image of God as we think of human images; the word *image* cannot refer to God's physical image because He is absolute in constitution and devoid of visible properties. But knowing that God is a Spirit and spirits don't have solid properties must not diminish our desire to learn what *image* means in the context of Creation. While the meaning of the *image* of God is inconceivable, the corporation of the Godhead in Creation may shed light on how we can understand His presentiments of image. The Trinity is united under God; God spoke the Word, and His Spirit moved upon the firmaments.

In the beginning, God, His Word, and His Spirit were distinct but distinctly one. This precludes what would have been a normal search for the definition of *Godhead.* To understand what is intended as image, let us review what we generally conceive as the image of God and pursue it for clarity along these discourses.

In all the previous developmental cycles to grace, there was no distinct mention of a triune God. The Hebrew Scripture said, "Hear Oh Israel the Lord our God is one Lord." Hebraic theology presented Yahweh as the one true God. However, despite the omission or lack of a triune God, in the early cycles, we were privileged with what biblical scholars call theophanies, pre-manifestations of the Messiah. In Daniel 3:25 (KJV), Nebuchadnezzar said, "Lo, I see four men loose, walking in the midst of the fire, and they have no hurt; and the form of the fourth is like the Son of God."

"In the beginning was the Word, and the Word was with God, and the Word was God. He was with God in the beginning. Through him all things were made; without him nothing was made that has been made" (John 1:1–3 KJV). These words define the participation of Jesus in the Genesis account of Creation, but they also refer to the distinctness of the Son. God said, "Let," and His Spirit obeyed God's mandate. This unquestionably divulges the precreation presence of the Lord's sonship, the Savior working in total harmony in creation. We have increased our understanding of the Spirit's participation, and this strengthens our conceptualization of God's image. Through this study, we have seen that God is a triune being, so it must be that *image* refers to our bodies, souls, and spirits.

We have our first total manifestation of the order in the Godhead in Jesus' baptism by John the Baptist. The Son amenably committed Himself to the will of the Father in baptism, and we were blessed with the first appearance of the Spirit of God; He descended from heaven in the form of a dove and lit upon the Lord. It had been declared to John that he would see a dove descend upon His Son. While others may have thought they had heard thunder, a voice from heaven said, "This is my beloved Son, hear him." This is indeed a genuine revelation of the triune personhood of God.

> And Jesus, when he was baptized, went up straightway out of the water: and, lo, the heavens were opened unto him, and he saw the Spirit of God descending like a dove, and lighting upon him: And lo a voice from heaven, saying, This is my beloved Son, in whom I am well pleased. (Matthew 3:16–17 KJV)

I am not attempting to draw distinctions in the Godhead or explain the doctrine of the Trinity, but we have a clear image of the Godhead here. As the Son was being baptized, the Spirit in the form of a dove lit upon Him and God spoke. This is enough proof for me to conclude that there are three persons in the Trinity and that I was created in His image.

This information is essential to our understanding of the triune image of humanity that identifies it with its Maker. We can hardly expect to understand the creation of man without understanding the unique aspects of the Trinity. We are taught that Jehovah fabricated us from dust. This is mesmerizing; though other creatures' bodies decompose to dust, there is no information about their physical construction. This knowledge certainly helps explain the image concept of the Creator and His creation. This is the only visible distinguishing contrast between the Creator and His creation. God needed something physical to make us with. Every physical creature requires a body, but we are more complex than are other creatures; we also possess a spirit and an immortal soul. Though we were made by a triune God, it was a collaborative process.

Up to this point in the creation progression, all visible images were the result of the performance of the Word, but God did something beyond just speaking humanity into existence. Here, we learn of the first time God was directly involved in the creation process by saying "Let us." Prior to that, God had said, "Let there be," and it was so according to His Word's creative power. But making "us" involved the collaboration of the Trinity. The Genesis account states that God created us in His likeness and image, but the authentication of the unity of the Trinity was not fully revealed until Jesus' baptism.

God formed man from the dust of the earth. This earthen formation is critically significant. Our creation from dust establishes man an earth bound or terrestrial beings; this is the only direct connection we have to our environment and other earthly inhabitants. Our likeness and image are different from that of any other creature.

Likeness includes an identity with deity and encompasses the perfect distinctiveness of God's character. Our characteristics are essentially God's. Whatever elements constituted his psychological being, they were similar to God's. In other words, we were the recipients of all the lower attributes of God required to make us perfect and unique beings. He created us completely moral and sinless beings in a terrestrial world. Our attributes though puerile were perfect.

Chapter 4

What Really Happened in Eden

> And the serpent said unto the woman, Ye shall not surely die:
> For God doth know that in the day ye eat thereof, then your eyes shall be opened, and ye shall be as gods, knowing good and evil. (Genesis 3:4–5 KJV)

We may begin this study by being conscientiously aware that Adam and Eve enjoyed; and their first years on earth were in the absolute bliss, glorious innocence in a utopian environment all to themselves. However, their other intelligent neighbor wasn't just their Creator and mentor, who came and fellowshipped with them. As we seek to draw closer to our first parents to learn what really happened, we must try to see them through a solidified psychological as well as a spiritual relationship. Otherwise, we could run the risk of making the mistake of forgetting they were real human beings. We must not ignore the fact that they exhibited human tendencies. It would be inconceivable to believe they were given a free will without a healthy portion of emotions as well as free will.

Emotions can easily control our free will. From what we have learned about God's strong desire to establish relationships with His children, we can only assume that Adam and Eve's interactions with Him had all the essential qualities of genuine free will and emotions. Where his children are concern, God's response is never casual in His dealings with us. These encounters most certainly must have been inconceivably ingratiating experiences of delight: Nirvana.

Their meetings with God must have been glorious compared to our chance encounters with Him in this depleted world in which His presence is almost completely obscured by the heinous intrusion of selfishness and sin. We are famished for intimate encounters with Him amid the blights of sin and decay. Imagine the bliss of unobscured and uninterrupted fellowship with Him! Without the risking reaching too far, to look seriously at what really happened in Eden and to learn if human emotions came to bear on these unimaginable encounters, we must keep a spiritual and physical mind-set when we evaluate our forebears.

The tragedy that resulted in the fall was the result of Satan's skillful handling of desire. He used it to create misunderstanding and fuel a deep desire for God. What this amounted to was a destructive and intrusive violation of Adam and Eve's sovereignty. The seduction of desire led Eve astray. You may detest Satan's insinuation that orchestrated Adam and Eve's selfish desire, but it led to their deaths. He drained Eve's affection of its genuine desire and told her how intelligent she could become. All that was basically true, but it wasn't how God had planned to educate His children.

Could Eve have been a good student? No! A great and an engaging student caught up in the charisma of an endearing heavenly Father? She was rendered oblivious to the things her enemy had told her. Completely submersed in the thought of pleasing her Creator, she hung onto Satan's lies. Somewhat like we ourselves who are given over to prayer, meditation, and fasting to draw closer to Him.

We don't know God's reasons for visiting the garden, but His presence is the fullness of joy. We must draw from what we know of the influence of the Holy Spirit on the human psyche and use the simpler frame of reference to understand Eve's logic. Real Christians have a strong desire to patronize their Patron. This appeasement is not condescending; it's cultivated out of loyalty due to the blessings, concerns, and interests shown to us by our heavenly Father.

Girls seem to have a greater sense of embracing admiration for their fathers. Behavioral scientists stress this point to demonstrate how such relationships can sometimes become toxic. Of course that's a stretch, but based on what we just discussed, could it be that Eve sought greater knowledge and perfection so she could communicate more intelligently and intimately with her Creator? This is not unheard of. We are sometimes awestruck by just the sheer dynamics of one word from God. And just to hear that one word, don't we fast, pray, and meditate to get closer to Him because we want to be more intimate with Him? If these ideas are credible assessments of our emotional needs, we must understand Eve wasn't a drone—she had these feelings too. She thought she was capable of feeling great, pure passion for her Father, but she wasn't told how to manage her emotions. That's one of the blights of free will.

If Eden was an incubatory sanctuary, we can see why it might have been natural for her to want to emulate her Dad. Seeing that apart from her husband, He was the only other person around is a huge plus to this theory. Her wishes to rise above her present status were real and rightly hers to seek so she could communicate with God more intellectually and effectively. We'd do the same if we could.

We find this sentiment imbedded in the Sinaic Laws: "Thou shall love the Lord thy God with All thy heart." A lack of desire and commitment is a tremendous problem even in today's congregations. People say they love God, but many give that sentiment only lip service. They show no passion for the presence of God or retain Him in their consciences. As a pastor, I've had firsthand experiences with people who must be amused and entertained until they're emotionally heightened enough to engage in praise and worship.

It's a calamity when desires supersede knowledge. Someone comes along who calls himself a prophet and prophesies a ten-dollar prophecy, something that's only cosmetically pretty, one from the catalog of alluring promises. Before some people even understand what's being said, their emotions take control because it sure sounds provocative.

Many Christian brothers and sisters with good intentions and great potential have been destroyed through renegade desires. For this reason, these fantastic prophecies, people are ready to leave church and home; they can no longer be content with the fellowship they are in because their mental comfort has been usurped. That may sound crazy, but it happens all the time; unchecked emotions are dangerous feelings.

At one time or another, it seemed that everyone was writing a book or a sermon on the mind. A major concern about this battlefield is that although many are harping about the battlefield, no one offers any plausible solution for buttressing the emotional outbursts that accompany so wide a spirituality. Some may be able to identify emotional reactions, but they come up short every time.

God knows exactly how to bring us along developmentally, and unwarranted interruptions could seriously compromise our spiritual maturity. God had an in-depth regiment of activities He designed to help Adam and Eve along ever so meticulously.

Jacob's night stop at Bethel and his vision there of a ladder reaching into heaven confirms for us that nothing just happens. God is at work in unseen situations; He knows the way we take. In Hebrews, Paul described the Lord Jesus Christ as the author and finisher of our faith. It is not a happenstance outline with arbitrary events.

Satan's strategy in this first temptation was an openly hostile aggression against Eve; he, the prince of subtleties, wanted to usurp God's plan and continue to rebel against God out of resentment. He wanted to counter Eve's love for her Father caused by her desire for Him. He deceived her into believing she could achieve a likeness and knowledge of God ahead of schedule.

She was unaware of the danger of acquiring knowledge without experience and maturity. That can lead to dire consequences; wanting full rights to free will can be catastrophic. The quest of absolute free will can result in complete alienation from God and is sin. The Bible entreated us to not rely on our own understanding but to acknowledge God as the designer and the provider of providence. God is not checked by free will. Though God will not supersede free will for His glory, He will do so on behalf of others and on our own behalf.

"For the scripture saith unto Pharaoh, Even for this same purpose have I raised thee up, that I might shew my power in thee, and that my name might be declared throughout all the earth" (Romans 9:17 KJV). God purposefully created Pharaoh to demonstrate His power. The prophet said that as clay was in the hands of the potter, so was Israel in God's hands. The authority of God is uncheckable; in Hosea, He said, "He does as he please, He is God." But to better understand God's sovereignty, let's go back to our observation of God interacting with the king of Egypt.

> Then Pharaoh called for Moses and Aaron in haste; and he said, I have sinned against the LORD your God, and against you. Now therefore forgive, I pray thee, my sin only this once, and intreat the LORD your God, that he may take away from me this death only. (Exodus 10:16–17 KJV)

Can you believe God said no? His will be done. God made an example out of him. More than demonstrating His power, He demonstrated that disobedience to His will was catastrophic. The Word says, "Disobedience is as the sin of witchcraft." The perils of leaning to our own understanding are ominous. Behind his satanic prodding was the idea that if Satan could entice Adam and Eve to pursue their godliness prematurely, he could derail their journey to dominion, thus regaining something he so desperately wanted.

To tell them they wouldn't die was a great negligence of the truth. The misunderstanding came under the idea of "wouldn't surely." God and Satan were speaking of the same thing but from different points of view. The flesh profits nothing; it is the Spirit that gives life. Death according to God is something He has no say over. As He told Israel, "Choose this day whom you will serve." Although this choice may be undermined, it is ultimately up to us. When sin is conceived, it brings forth death. We must understand that the absence of God's life in us is real death and separation from God. No one is alive spiritually without the life of God in him or her. The fall was actually the breath God breathed into Adam and Eve draining out.

The other scenario contains imperatives, but they can be seen easily from the extent to which we live in our fallen state. Righteous folk may fall seven times, but God will raise them. Physical death is only a beginning in another place and time. Satan uses this misunderstanding even among us today despite the Word admonishing us to weep when we come into the world and rejoice when we leave this world.

Satan may have scored a victory when Eve ate and didn't drop to the ground and realized the difference between good and evil. Job said God gives two and three warnings before He sends us to the pit. That statement comes into play when we raise the question of Eve's knowledge of death. Job said He delivers enough warning before He tempers His prerogatives of mercy and judgment. These early cycles of development are filled with incidents of uncertainty. From the teaching of the Bible, we have learned that the Lord always tempers judgment with warnings before He administers destruction.

Satan's chief goal has been and continues to be to get us to act independently of God's will. Evidence of his deception is throughout Scripture. At the wedding in Cana, the deceiver goaded Jesus' mother to rouse Him to act before it was His time. She became so involved in forcing Jesus to display His power though He made it clear it wasn't His time.

Satan's contemptuous disregard for the Lord in the temptations in the wilderness was a more blatant intrusion. Satan does not always tell nasty lies; he mixes truth into them. He contrives deceits to manipulate situations to his advantage by shifting our focus. This was a big part of the undertone in the wilderness temptations. Nothing he said to the Lord was a glaring lie; he knew it was impossible to get the Lord to act out of ignorance of the Word, so he tried to manipulate Jesus to act according to the Word. His design was to sway the Lord into validating His credentials out of His contempt and disdain for Satan.

The Lord and Satan knew Jesus was the Messiah. Prophesies meticulously outlined the hardship the Messiah would have to endure to be truly credited as the Lamb of God that took away the sins of the world. Satan seemingly wanted to ease the perils Jesus would suffer on His path to establishing His kingdom, so Satan offered Him a way to messiahship with no bloodshed. But no bloodshed was a heinous exclusion; without it, there is no remission of sin. This beast still pushes this message through the church today; many churches no longer speak of blood-washed saints.

When Satan said, If you are the Son of God ..." he wasn't suggesting he didn't know who Jesus was or was casting doubt on the Lord's sonship. This intimation was like the ploy he had perpetrated on Eve. It was not intended to make our Savior doubt but to seduce Him into acting out of the confidence that He was who He claimed to be. A miracle would be the proper credential that would authenticate his sonship.

Satan's rhetorical question was designed to embolden Him to act out of self-will against the will of His Father and demonstrate He was the Christ. Any action of this nature would have sabotaged His messiahship. Nothing would have been achieved through disobedience to the Father. Jesus was capable of sinning but was sinless. There is no way I would believe that the Lord would have even considered Satan's scheme. This is not to undermine the severity of the temptation; I know other things apart from the beating and the physical death mustered serious attention. But Satan would have had to contrive a more plausible avenue than pride in Himself to get Jesus' attention. Jesus was not acting as God; He was God. He was the Son of Man created for this purpose alone.

Satan's offering our Lord the keys to the kingdom of the world was an attempt to seduce Him into making unholy allegiances with the popular movements of the day: the Pharisees, Sadducees, Herodias, and the other heretics of that time. In that way, Jesus could forgo the shedding of blood, the nailing of the ordinances that were against us, the humiliation of the cross, and the cruelty He would receive at the hands of His people. It would supposedly shortcut having to take back the keys of death, hell, and the grave. This was a flawed supposition mainly because the enemy employed the same deception used against Eve. These strategies have proven strategic and productive in the past, but no matter how he tried to disguise his intent, it would have been apparent to the Lord.

The Lord did only those things that pleased His Father. He told His disciples that He could have sent for ten legions of angels and have aborted the plan of salvation, that He could do whatever He pleased. Blood sacrifice was a critical part of our restoration process; without the shedding of blood, there is no remission for sin. The Lord was not going along in his messianic appearance playing it by ear. At the tender age of twelve, seventeen years before the temptation in the desert, He was in the temple at Jerusalem confounding the doctors. During that time, He reminded His mother it was time He went about his Father's business.

By subtle measures, Satan encouraged Eve to pursue her desire to be like her Father. He wanted her in direct contravention of God's mandate.

> And the LORD God commanded the man, saying, Of every tree of the garden thou mayest freely eat: But of the tree of the

knowledge of good and evil, thou shalt
not eat of it: for in the day that thou eatest
thereof thou shalt surely die. (Genesis
1:16–17 KJV)

It would seem ridiculous to say that you would die
if you ate of the Tree of Life, but I think this command
referred also to the Tree of Life though it wasn't directly
included in the admonition. The Tree of Life was not
mentioned because it might have been impossible to
get to it without the knowledge from the Tree of the
Knowledge of Good and Evil. This appears to be a
valid thought based on the concept of training in Eden.

Behavioral scientists emphasize the necessity of
fully embracing the developmental stages humans go
through from infancy to adulthood. I'm not suggesting
the Eden cycle was a paradigm for maturity, but I
believe it was a requisite for eternal life. For one, it's
foolish to suggest it's possible to develop a life of piety
without a mature conscience.

The haunting behavior of adults who didn't or
weren't permitted to embrace life's developmental
stages is emblematic of deficient growth. We find
these people among society's permanent misfits.
Their functionality has been marred by the absence of

trials and errors during their growth stages. They are adult children and are at best socially dysfunctional. They have difficulty coping with life's challenges and can't manage their emotions or their lives. People who didn't achieve maturity through these sequential steps are often those who live very unpredictable lives.

The tempter knew the consequences of his deception because he at one time tried to supersede God and was relegated to the firmament indefinitely. Satan didn't tell an accusative lie; if he had, Eve would have seen through his intent. His deceit came in the form of a concoction of lies intermingled with some truth. Satan doesn't know what's in our minds, so he must have heard their conversation on this subject. I don't suggest anything about what Adam and Eve might have talked about after Jehovah's visit, but it seems he knew Eve's desire, which helped him tempt her with precision by his subtle distortion of the truth. He perverted God's command to Adam from a stern warning to something seemingly desirable and fitting. God said, "You would surely die," but Satan said, "You will not surely die; you will become better for your effort."

After securing Eve's attention, he unfolded an elaborate proposal. His plan was an immediate rebuttal of Eve's statement; instead of directly addressing her concerns, he appealed to what he sensed she desired most but without an accusative undertone. He told her, "For God doth know that in the day ye eat thereof, then your eyes shall be opened, and ye shall be as gods, knowing good and evil." This is true, but he didn't mention the ramifications of disobeying God's will he had firsthand knowledge about. He baited the trap with the promise of instantaneousness delight if she ate the fruit. He promised her that she would visit with God as His equal. He realized he couldn't tempt Adam and Eve by revealing his disdain for God; they wouldn't have tolerated that. But Satan knew he could appeal to their desire to be like their heavenly benefactor. He tempted them to seek appointment as if they were already mature enough to be gods. They were evicted from Eden though they were only infants spiritually, but God covered them, and the Spirit continued His guidance even in the blackest moments.

We must address two ideas before we can look further. We read in Genesis 3:22 KJV, "And the Lord God said, Behold, the man is become as one of us, to know good and evil: and now, lest he put forth his hand, and take also of the tree of life, and eat, and live forever." Some say God spoke caustically here while others say it was in deep consideration. Some scholars believe the original reading to be wrong. These scholars seem to assume the Edenic couple must have had a functioning level of conscience even if their reasoning process was matured only to an extent. It's reasonable to assume they were conscious enough to know not to disobey God. There is no proof they understood what death meant, and yet we are hard pressed to believe God would give mandates before any clarification. So we must conclude that the mere fact that they were forbidden by God to eat from the Tree of the Knowledge of Good and Evil is not enough to indicate they had contact with conscience, the ability to reason logically to discover right and wrong. This would not ready them for valid logical reasoning.

Chapter 5

The Lamp of God

> The spirit of man is the candle of the
> LORD. Proverbs 20:27 (KJV)

> For what is a man profited, if he shall gain
> the whole world, and lose his own soul?
> or what shall a man give in exchange for
> his soul? Matthew 16:26 (KJV)

This lesson of our Lord requires us to determine the soul's value. The Lord's intention here might seem obvious, but a careful consideration reveals that the Lord is calculating. What is clear, however, is His emphasis on the inviolability of the soul. Our uncertainty is with the question raised in this statement, which seems to suggest that the soul is more valuable than all the world's wealth. We will discover the soul's value, but first, we must decide for whom the soul is so invaluable the second part of the question seems to be rhetorical. Its primary purpose is to accentuate the sentiments of the question.

Some scholars suggest that the Bible uses the words *soul* and *spirit* interchangeably. On the surface, this seems to be the case, but this has created uncertainty. The different meanings have produced a series of points of entry to the definition: words such as *living being*, *life*, *self*, *person*, *desire*, *appetite*, *emotion*, *passion*, and *breath* have blended to darken and obscure the meaning of the word *soul*.

Many insubstantial definitions create ambiguity in the meaning of the word *soul*. Arriving at a safe definition upon which we agree may require narrowing our search to include only biblical definitions to complement our primary interest. However, a number of classic philosophers have contributed greatly to the overall meaning of the word. A study of philosophy would give you a broader knowledge of the subject.

Soul in Hebrew is *nephesh* and in Greek is *psyche.* I take this interchangeability into consideration in this work, but we must ensure that both words have the same sense. Getting a handle of the Hebrew definition seems to be the most complicated because there are variations in synonyms. There is only one word for *soul* in the gospel; knowing this would make our inquiry easier, but the Hebrew Scripture has a wider range of synonyms for nephesh. As well, in many places, the words *spirit* and *soul* are used interchangeably. This poses concern because it would prove inaccurate and wouldn't corroborate the interpretation in grace.

Man was created a triune being—body, soul, and spirit. Jehovah breathed His breath into the nostril of man to make him a living soul. Though none of the uses of *soul* in the gospel is translated "spirit," the Hebraic interchangeability of these word makes the interpretation reasonable. The Hebrew scriptural root word for spirit is *ruach*, and the gospel root word for spirit is *pneuma.* However, both nephesh and ruach have been translated "breath" in some renditions in Hebrew Scripture.

> I looked, and tendons and flesh appeared on them and skin covered them, but there was no breath in them. Then said he unto me, "Prophesy, son of man, and say to it, 'this is what the Sovereign Lord says: Come, breath from the four winds and breathe into these slain, that they may live.'" So I prophesied as he commanded

me, and breath entered them; they came to life and stood up on their feet. (Ezekiel 37:8–10 KJV)

Here, the prophet used all four representation of nephesh: breath, wind, life, and spirit for good reason. First, wind in the gospel and Hebrew literature means spirit, but only in Hebrew does it means soul as well. Breath means soul and breathe means life. Obedient to the command of Jehovah, the prophet followed the command of God, who released His Spirit, His soul, and as He did to our Edenic parents, with His breath, He breathed life into the bones. This is a preferable rendering; it indicates how Jehovah refreshed the dry bones, the dead soul of a dead spirit.

A close look at the Hebrew text suggests that the usages of these words can be categorized three ways. I suggest arranging the interpretations this way because each way is specific in terms of clarifying a unique concept of the human spirit. The general list of synonyms consists of the following words for soul: *living being* and *person*; *desire, emotion*, and *passion*; and *appetite* and *throat*. Treating the definitions and connotations in these categories narrows the point of view and strengthens the meaning. This also allows us to reason from a concrete base to determine why there is such a huge list of synonyms for *soul*.

The extent of these many meanings is basically from Hebrew scriptural usage and interpretation. Synthesizing the many renderings into one conception would prove much more worthwhile than trying to deal with them individually. The grouping of the different substitution for the word *soul* is intended to define its various natures, the application of that nature to the whole being, and its lesser and higher functions.

Our first series includes living beings and persons; this list seems to introduce the thought of the lesser life, the terrestrial life of humanity. "And shall consume the glory of his forest, and of his fruitful field, both soul and body: and they shall be as when a standard bearer fainteth" (Ezekiel 37:8–9 KJV). Here, the prophet Isaiah wrote of "both soul and body" interchangeably; it seems his basic intention was to not distinguish between the upper and lesser life in the living being. He seemed to focus on their end, their utter destruction, their ability to be completely consumed. This Scripture is understood to mean that human beings are made up of the soul and the flesh that can both be utterly consumed. This is difficult, because if we're being directed to believe this is the prophet's understanding of the soul, there is a great discrepancy between his view and our goal. It would better serve us to understand the prophet to mean that the body and soul could be permanently destroyed only by hell—alienation from the life of God. This is in keeping with the eternality of the soul.

This idea is in line with other renditions of this thought in Hebraic literature. In Leviticus 17:11 (KJV), we read, "For the life of the flesh is in the blood: and I have given it to you on the altar to make an atonement for your souls: for it is the bold that makes an atonement for the soul." Jehovah draws upon the higher life form of the being, the blood. This interpretation can be extended to include the major teaching on atonement and sacrifice. Here, Jehovah built the idea that the life of the being's flesh was in the blood, which contains the soul. The general idea here is that by consuming a beast's blood, its soul is being consumed. This should help greatly in clarifying why the blood shouldn't be consumed—it constitutes the soul of the creature.

> Therefore will I divide him a portion with the great, and he shall divide the spoil with the strong; because he hath poured out his soul unto death: and he was numbered with the transgressors; and he bare the

sins of many, and made intercession for the transgressors. (Isaiah 53:12 KJV)

This verse is a prophetic reference to Jesus Christ. Many translations have used "life," "spirit," "soul," and "blood" interchangeably to refer to the pouring out of His soul. It's clear, however, that Jehovah teaches us that the soul is in the blood. Isaiah 53:12 (KJV) has all the rings of the messianic atonement on the cross, where He poured out His blood, His life, His nephesh. We can now understand that Christ bled and died; His soul for our soul. This was the medium to pay for our transgressions. Without the shedding of blood, there is no remission of sin, which when conceived brings death. The soul that sins will surely die; this death is the absence of the breath of God.

Nephesh is also rendered "desire," "emotion," "self," and "passion." These renditions draw the characteristics of the soul closer to the general concept of the person. In Isaiah 5:14 (KJV) and Habakkuk 2:5 (KJV), nephesh is translated "desire" and "appetite." This concept also applies to the lesser life where throat can mean breath, an instrument of breathing, but also means appetite and desire. In Isaiah 5:1 (KJV) and 32:6 (KJV), it's rendered "the seat of appetite and desire." Appetites and desires are the driving forces behind the self. If left unchecked, they can result in reprobation.

In the gospel, the Greek word *psyche* is used over a hundred times. Apart from the general term *soul*, which occurs more than fifty-five times as psyche, it is also used to refer to the self, heart, and life. *Psyche* is applied to the essential nature of the soul, it introduces the idea of a holistic being of body, soul, and spirit. In short, nephesh and psyche identify the nature and importance of the soul, the totality of the spirit person, the center of life, emotions, feelings, and longings. It is the invaluable seat of the kingdom of Christ in the believer, the immortality in the nature of humanity. All are born spiritually dead because of the transgression of Adam and Eve. "Thou hidest thy face, they are troubled; thou takest away their breath, they die and return to dust" (Psalms 104:29 KJV).

Let us try to understand why a human spirit has to be lit by the breath, the ruach of God to become a soul, the spirit, soul, and candle of humanity. Those who consider the spirit as the rational soul perhaps have in view the essential nature of the soul, conscience, desire, emotion, and passion. This seems to be a good analysis of the rational soul because the fall rendered the soul of man stripped of all these qualities.

The inward part literally mean "belly" in Habakkuk 2:5 KJV; which is translated appetite and desire; but which closes with the expression "searching the inward parts of the belly." This translation may render belly as "soul," which literally mean "desire" and "appetite."

Since we were all born into sin as a consequence of the fall, all human souls are dead and depleted of their vital characteristics. We are born brute, dead in sin before the illumination. This death literally means the extinguishing of the candle, which represents the awakening to consciousness and reasoning. The extinguishment of the glorious illumination of the soul once lit by the breath of the Almighty and the awakening to consciousness and reasoning.

Jesus told Nicodemus, "That which is born of flesh is flesh and that which is born of Spirit is spirit." (John 3:6 KJV) And what is spirit is spirit and will remain spirit. He clearly distinguished the two natures in this statement and set them supernaturally apart. A clear definition of a lesser life is suggested by flesh, and a higher intellectual life is suggested by the spirit. Jesus was not suggesting that flesh and spirit were interchangeable; their coming together can be only through the illumination of God's breath, the greatest of all miracles.

In this teaching on the soul, our Lord placed great emphasis on the priceless measure of the soul. He suggested there was nothing sensual that could be measured equivalent to the soul, that it was priceless. Through a series of recurring questions. He demonstrates that it has no equal. "What had a man to profit if he gained the world?"

In St. Mark's Gospel, chapter eight (KJV), Jesus taught a critical lesson on the value of the soul in two rhetorical questions: He effectively defined its incomparability, "For what shall it profit a man, if he shall gain the whole world, and lose his own soul? Or what shall a man give in exchange for his soul?" These questions underpinned two central messages our Lord wished to get across to us on the value of the soul. In these lessons He presents spiritual, as well as sensual implications on the incompatibility of the soul.

The first question seems to emphasize the importance of intellectual and worldly achievements, He asked, "For what is a man profited, if he shall gain the whole world, and lose his own soul? Or what shall a man give in exchange for his soul" when we look at high and coveted academics' success that are all his to gain and the wealth of power and success that accompanies them; even the prominence and prestige of positions contrived by knowledge. The Bible emphasizes with profound clarity that the wisdom of this world is foolishness to those who perish. This statement fits well with the Lord's choice of servants in His kingdom; not many nobles or wise people are called. He uses the foolish things of this world to confound the wise that no flesh might glory.

Although, there was no indication that the church of Laodicea was in mind in this thought process, the tone is highly suggestive of great worldly success. That is the substance that sums up the mentality of the Laodicean church and it seems to be well inside the boundaries of Christian teaching. The accolades that would certainly be required for highly prestigious appointments to great gubernatorial and senatorial positions are the wealth of the world, and even the accoutrements of stardom have prominent places in worldly wealth. Meanwhile, knowledge can secure chief seats and the praises of others but not the salvation of a soul. This is all head knowledge and therefore cannot illuminate the soul, which is the impartation of spiritual life. The wisdom of this world is foolishness to those who perish. The soul is immortal, and nothing sensual and mortal can improve its fallen, depraved condition.

The second question the Lord asked addressed the spiritual aspect of worldly achievements: "Or what shall a man give as an exchange for his soul?" Even after we have acquired the riches of a substantial academic enterprise from the service of your Gubernatorial, Senatorial or stardom tenure; but even in this, the proceeds of wealthy possession remains inadequate in measure up to the quality of the soul.

We see this teaching illustrated more clearly in the parable Jesus told of a man whose fields had yielded a substantial harvest. He sought to secure his products and live a happy life on the produce, so to speak. He died; his soul was required of him. The Lord said he had been a fool because he had sought to provide only for the body and had ignored his soul. Spiritually and physically, nothing can match the value of the soul.

We must be born again to acquire or be gifted a living soul. The Word says, "Therefore if any man be in Christ, he is a new creature: old things are passed away; behold, all things are become new." 2 Corinthians 5:17 KJV) When we are born again, our soul is transferred out of the kingdom of the darkness of ignorance and into the kingdom of light through the illuminating breath of God. Christ is the Word, the wisdom of God. He is light that illuminates the hearts of every man that cometh into the world. Those who are born again not of the flesh, but of the Spirit.

Major commentaries have misinterpreted this verse. I don't mean to criticize the distinguished writers of Bible commentaries, the point and fact to this alluding rest specifically on the need to distinguish the nature and characteristics of the soul. Before Adam and Eve left Eden, they were reduced to the level of brutes. Although their primary functions were not instinctive, they were practically equivalent to instinct. They had been evicted from the kingdom of Jehovah and were dead in trespasses and sin, the abandonment Jesus experienced on the cross. A gorge of separation sustained the alienation. He cried, "My God, My God why had thou forsaken me?" He who knew no sin had become sin. Consequently, by the time Adam and Eve departed Eden, they were no longer triune beings. The fall had stripped them of intellect and morality. Most significant in this degenerate state was the loss of the likeness and image of God had placed in them at creation.

> Then the Lord God formed a man from
> the dust of the ground and breathed into
> his nostrils the breath of life, and the man

became a living soul. And out of the ground the LORD God formed every beast of the field, and every fowl of the air; and brought them unto Adam to see what he would call them: and whatsoever Adam called every living creature, that was the name thereof. (Genesis 2:7, 19 KJV)

There is no evidence that after the creation of man he was inanimate until the Creator's breath animated him; his higher life came from God's breath. So to suggest that the breath of the Almighty gave both lower and higher life could not be substantiated. The account in Genesis 2:19 (KJV) is analogous to verse 7. The creation of man and the creation of brutes are similar to an extent. After the creation of the physical body of the brutes from the ground, they had a life force; they were designed to act instinctively. This was a lower life form; it lacked critical, life-sustaining communication such as logical, conscientious reasoning abilities.

The major distinguishing feature between lower and higher life forms is free will. At his creation, God breathed into his nostrils, and man became a living soul capable of reasoning and emotions. He gave this higher form the ability to make choices. In this book, we will try to discover the prerequisite for permission to eat from the Tree of the Knowledge of Good and Evil. This depended on Adam and Eve's reasoning abilities during their time of innocence.

The lesser life form, the brutes, had instincts that allowed them to make complex and specific responses based on environmental stimulations without involving reason. These tendencies originate and function below the conscious level. Instinct is the opposite of reasoning. God did not give man instincts; otherwise, He could not have given him free choice. The higher life form has the ability to supersede nature. We don't mate in the fall and build nests in the spring so that we synchronize our children's births with the ripening of berries.

Scripture does however teach that there is a higher and a lesser life form in man. When God breathed into man, he became a living soul. The breath of the Almighty is the distinguishing element between verse 7 and verse 19. It set man apart as a unique life form by granting him a soul, God breathes into man and a soul is animated. The soul is the meeting place of God in man. The ministries of God to man transpire in the soul. The breath is the illuminator of God. We clearly understand why our soul is called the lamp of God.

The soul is a vessel that must contain some form of flammable, and by God's process, it can be lit; this is the beginning of the elevation of the human psyche.

Breath always means life, and it is also true when it applies to our heavenly Father. There are two very critical concepts of the soul we must understand clearly here. First, the soul is the seat of reasoning, thoughts, desires, affections, and will. Second, it is the place of conscience in humans. Conscience includes a number of essential intellectual concepts such as the perception of right from wrong and their attendant feelings of joy or sorrow; the judgment of a particular action as being right or wrong; the feeling of pleasure or compunction which follows right and wrong actions. The illuminated soul is under the intellectual supervision of God; its chief purpose is to search out and control our spiritual functions. It is the seat of the governing principle; it accuses or excuses the choices we make. "The spirit of man is the candle of the LORD, searching all the inward parts of the belly" (Proverbs 20:27 KJV).

There is a lower form of life in man, we have already discussed his higher form. Although we cannot accurately place the point of origin of humanity's lower form, but we are certain all humans are born with a spirit but because of the fall, they were born in sin and shaped in iniquity. They are rendered spiritually dead and therefore do not possess an illuminated spirit.

Proverbs 27:19 (KJV) tells us, "As in water face answereth to face, so the heart of man to man the unregenerate heart is dead."

In this verse from the Proverbs we understand the heart of man answers to the heart of man, or soul, nephesh. The soul is dead; it is devoid of conscience. There is a knowledge of what is transpiring inside the heart, but the will to override the demands of the flesh is weak. The specific performance of the soul has been relegated the task of controlling sensual reasoning. This is what the apostle Paul meant when he expressed the despondent sentiments of an inner struggle in an unregenerate heart. We have already established that humanity does not have instinct; however, their actions may seem instinctual at times because they are incapable of elevating their conscience. So the deeds of one debauched person resemble the deeds of all miscreants with corrupt natures.

Just as true believers reflect Christ, so do those who share in the fallen heritage. This may not be a pleasing proverb, but sinners do what sinners do.

Their desires correspond to the desires of each other. They cannot receive the things of God and therefore cannot make right moral decisions; they behave the same in action and thought, which resembles instinct.

When Adam and Eve fell from grace and fellowship with God, they were spiritually dead; their lamps were out. The Holy Spirit had left the building, and they had lost their God-given ability to make appropriate decisions. When Jehovah breathed into the nostril of man, he was made a living soul; he was like his heavenly Creator. We have concluded that based on the Edenic incubatory development theory, the illumination the Spirit afforded man gave him the ability to communicate with his Creator astutely enough to be able to have fellowship. If it had not been extinguished, this would have evolved into perceptible intelligence. His soul was lit, and the wisdom of the Almighty resided in him; however, when the flame was snuffed out, his soul was left in darkness. He was pronounced spiritually dead.

From that point to Pentecost, no one was longer indwelled by the Holy Spirit. The Spirit came upon them or overshadowed them only for empowerment. Humanity's soul would remain in this fallen state until the Sun of Righteousness illuminated it. "But unto you that fear my name shall the Sun of righteousness arise with healing in his wings; and ye shall go forth, and grow up as calves of the stall" (Malachi 4:2 KJV).

This Sun of Righteousness resembles Christ, the fountain of light and life to the world. The Lord Jesus said, "I Am come that they might have life and that they might have it more abundantly." (John 10:10 KJV) He brings healing and deliverance through His teaching in the Spirit of truth and grace, which He promised to give His true followers and remove their ignorance and errors. He heals their starving souls, gives them spiritual health and strength, and restores their faculties and power.

Jesus declared Himself the light of the world, that which were to come, the light to lighten the hearts of humanity in the fullness of time had ran its course. In the temple at the great day of the feast, Jesus stood up and said, "I Am the Light of the world." (John 8:12 KJV) This surely must have touched the hearts of the pious worshipers there at the temple, for the huge chandelier of the temple was the symbol of the true light. No doubt that its rays cast the shadow of the Messiah throughout the room. The true light reflected their sins and guilt.

Chapter 6

God in the Dispensations

Biblical scholars divide the time of humanity into seven periods of differing lengths called dispensations by dispensationalists. I call them cycles because they are distinguishable by unique implementations of God's principles for creating growth in the human heart. These cycles usher in strategic changes in God's method of dealing with humanity or with some aspect of humanity in regard to two cases that bolster the necessity for humanity's development: the issues of sin and humanity's responsibility for it, and the restoration of dominion.

The cycles are progressive and distinguishable increments in humanity's maturation process on man. They are uniquely distinguishable by the identification of their principle factors and the identifiable testing apparatuses of human nature. Each of these governing principles helps appraise humanity's nature for change by the principal factor of the previous cycle. The duration of a cycle is determined by a prearranged extended time period of trial and error and ends with an assessment or judgment. Because of the specific purpose of the cycles, they do not overlap, but once the governing factor of a cycle has been introduced, progression to the next occurs.

Though the cycles are distinguishable periods and have been thus marked by unique events, they are in and of themselves not ultimately unique. God's purposes in them are for the good of humanity; they are built upon incrementally—a cycle is built upon by the preceding cycle.

God wants to teach men how to control and manage the domination of sin in their lives. This process is carried out through the establishment of a continuous maturation and development through which He defines His purposeful will. In response to these incremental improvements, a major role of ours is ultimate contribution to the matriculation through the progression as a threefold conformity, he must first believe, then secondly, he must obey and thirdly he must become. These lessons are thematic threads distinguishable throughout history. We can see our engagement with and implementation of these lessons through our will to obey Jehovah, the sign of growth.

Character change is a rite of passage, but even here, the application of the lessons determines where man's final destiny, where he will spend eternity. They may seem introductory and primitive, but they are not primal. These lessons are not prerequisites to a greater series of lessons; they are the core concepts of salvation we are to develop.

There is an overriding catastrophe in each of these cycles; the human drive to rebel against God is irreversible, and it appears impossible for humans to acclimate to the will of God. Our fallen nature seems to be so deeply marred by sin that we cannot maintain trust or belief in God or obey His will. Tragically, however, because of a lack of trust and belief, we are pulled from our Creator's hands. This regrettably has been the choices He exemplified in each dispensation.

Through countless pleas and call for repentance, God through his affirmative gestures continues to shine His love on us until we have rejected all His advances and requests for our obedience. He is longsuffering. Only after seasons of carefully orchestrated nurturing through appeals, trials, and errors does He pass judgment.

Grace is one of the chief corporate benefactions that is at work in each of the cycles. Some supposed that the advent of the Messiah, particularly his resurrection from the grave ushered grace. The Resurrection of Christ is generally thought to be the commencement of the cycle of grace perhaps because that was when subsidiary works of Christ were instituted. Through His atonement, grace derived a more significant meaning in this epoch.

Let us take a look at two of the major gifts which have been identified in grace. First, grace has freed God to interact with us intimately and personally, and secondly, it is the sum corollary of what Christ did. Grace authorizes the Father to benevolently bestow these gifts of grace on us. New Testament scholars define grace as the gift by which God is judiciously authorized, or is permitted to perform free and intimate acts of magnanimity on our behalf without any meretricious contributions on our part because Christ had been legally raised from the dead.

Grace, however, offers many more significant revelations. This cycle of human development offers for the first time the indwelling of the Spirit. It is the age of rebirth. It can also be termed the dispensation of grace because it is the epoch recognized as the fullness of time, which refers to. The fullness of time is generally regarded as the completion of the incubational cycles; it heralds the maturity of salvation, thus culminating in types, antitypes, and the advent of the Messiah.

The grandiosity of grace is found in granting the gift of eternal life by God, which had been sealed up in eternity from the collapse of Eden; it remained outside human consciousness until now. Jesus Christ the Lord gives everlasting life. When we look into the general advancement of the incubational evolvement, the presence the grace of God has always been the common significant factor in our spiritual evolution. We must understand that the presence of grace was always a significant imputation of God, and its presence has never diminished. The Messiah didn't usher in the era of grace; He ushered in a new epoch in the grace theme. In every dispensation, the grace of God has been the officious factor in our progression; it exemplifies God's loving, tender mercies. We have been the beneficiary of grace from creation. The interrelationship of grace and faith is the bolstering of every opportunity afforded man throughout history.

How do we track our spiritual progression to confirm that the dispensations are indeed developmental periods? We have already identified the commonality among them, the major threads that hold the periods together holistically. Here, we will look at how these periods differ, and take subjective glimpses at the unique concepts that explicate the exceptionality of the periods.

It's not my intention to teach dispensational truths; as I previously wrote, my only objective in touching on dispensational theories is to distinguish the developmental mechanism God uses at different stages of our maturation.

There are seven dispensations or cycles: innocence, conscience, government, promise, law, grace, tribulation, and kingdom. We will not concern ourselves with the millennium cycles.

The first of these cycles is innocence. All babies are thought to be innocent at birth, and this innocence is intended to include all creation. It was also meant to present the understanding that it was a sinless age, and innocence was its governing factor. It is the only time humanity embraced absolutely the image and likeness of the Creator.

Any speculation on the duration of any subsequent period is speculation I won't entertain in this book. I don't see the need for that type of knowledge and particularly any dogma on the matter.

Chapter 7

The Six Cycles

So God created mankind in his own image, in the image of God he created them; male and female he created them. God blessed them and said to them, "Be fruitful and increase in number; fill the earth and subdue it. Rule over the fish in the sea and the birds in the sky and over every living creature that moves on the ground."

Then God said, "I give you every seed-bearing plant on the face of the whole earth and every tree that has fruit with seed in it. They will be yours for food." Genesis 1:27–29 (KJV)

The Edenic Incubation

Man was created a perfect, sinless being. His Edenic tenure commenced with an uninterrupted exposure to an open communication with his Creator. This free access is considered the hallmark of the introduction to the Edenic developmental expectations. It is important, however, to give significant space to study other tasks that are identified, such as occupational and residency training rules that might have helped raise Adam and Eve.

Inside the garden, in which God placed the man and his wife, he created a little space; He called this garden within the garden Eden. Genesis 2:8 (KJV) "And the LORD God planted a garden eastward in Eden; and there he put the man whom he had formed" (Genesis 2:8 KJV). I am not suggesting that God was overprotective, however, we must give this isolated nook a bit of a serious second look because it gives us our first glimpse of the preparation Adam and Eve received a semblance of preparatory obligation being ministered to the couple.

They were delegated the responsibility to dress and subdue it. In other words, Adam was given caretaker-ship of a special place, not the whole Eden, but his own little rest bit. His tenure as God's man of dominion commenced inconspicuously. He named animals and plants and performed other prerogatives of juvenile acts of dominion in his innocence. Innocence can be characterized as the commencement of Adam's latent tenured itinerary. Scholars refer to the Adamic covenant as the covenant of works because of his principal assignments that. The performance of these activities ceased only when his innocence was interrupted through the fall. God closed the innocence cycle with the expulsion from Eden.

Here we see the manifestation of the first appearance of grace. The revelation of the gift of grace was given through the substitutionary sacrifice by God of an animal as atonement for the couple. The skin of the beast concealed their nakedness. They left Eden as mortals not that he wasn't previously, or at any other time God, but their latent likeness and image that they bore to their Creator was withdrawn, and the illumination went out rendering him permanently Homo sapiens.

Was this cycle completed? In other words, did it run the duration of its course? No. The premature fall of Adam permanently altered their growth pattern. Although, we may have only very little to go on in regard to the immediate function of the tree of life, and man's interaction with it, whether it was in the near foreseeable future, or it was not an activity destined to be interacted with, within the haven of Eden. The fall stopped any human activity in Eden that may have matured Adam and Eve in ways God was not pleased, demanding the immediate shutdown of any further activity that would expose man to other maturity activities in the boundary of Eden, in his debased state. God shut Eden down and placed guards at its gates to detour and discourage any further attempt of reentry. Adam was dismissed with only the skill of a farmer and a piece of skin on his back. I am not discriminating; I merely intend to establish humanity's capacity once outside Eden.

The next few verses in the chapter tell us that humanity's assignment could not have been intended for Eden alone; it applied to the whole earth. The activities assignment might be understood, but 'the face of the whole earth' cannot be rendered anything but outside the perimeter of the boundaries of the Adam Edenic: Utopia.

> And God said, Behold, I have given you
> every herb bearing seed, which is upon

the face of all the earth, and every tree, in the which is the fruit of a tree yielding seed; to you it shall be for meat. And to every beast of the earth, and to every fowl of the air, and to everything that creepeth upon the earth, wherein there is life, I have given every green herb for meat: and it was so. (Genesis 1:29–30 KJV)

Eden was the beginning of man's incubatory period because it was not anywhere else referred to as a type, caricature, or theory. The Lord tells us, "**Except ye** be converted, and **become** as little children, **ye** shall not enter into the kingdom of heaven." (Matthew 18:3 KJV) This startling command might appear as a vestige of Eden, but that should be considered only theoretical. Eden was a real place though scholars debate its location. The Bible has suggested its' proximity by highlighting various distinguishing landmarks features, such as mountains and rivers, but the exact location remains a mystery.

Adam had been given prerogatives over the whole earth, including seeds, a reference to the command to The presentation of seeds are always indicative of the process of second cause, which is associated with the nature of the first command to be fruitful and multiply. Despite his lofty and significant beginning, his authority was reduced to tilling, planting, and gathering. God mentioned that he would till the ground from whence he came. It might seem like amplification, but I detected an indictment of his physical nature, a staggering demotion. Farming was the vocation of Cain.

God revoked humanity's responsibility for the cultivation of dominion over creation, or the workmanship of gubernatorial-ship over everything that He had created. In verse 26, we read, "And let them have dominion over the fish of the sea, and over the fowl of the air, and over the cattle, and over all the earth, and over every creeping thing that crept upon the earth." Humanity needed knowledge of how to mature their characteristics to perform these arduous assignments. So in Eden, God planted a garden that Adam and Eve were to tend. It was not the world, nor was it a place for play; it was a restricted and reserved environment, a nursery in which God visited and began their growth matriculation. Verse 15 tells us, "And the Lord God took the man, and put him into the Garden of Eden to dress it and to keep it." Would innocence have been sufficient for God's intention for humanity? No. Knowledge was an essential necessity. The fall was the result of their disobedience to God. There can be no disobedience when there is no ultimatum. Our contention is not whether they had knowledge but how extensive that knowledge was.

God did not permit sin in order to establish knowledge as some have supposed. Nor did He create man to sin, the result of disobedience. Man was created a free moral agent; all his decisions were exclusively his, even to the extent of asking Jehovah for assistance, and the resulting consequences would be to his detriment.

Because Adam and Eve were infinitesimal in character advancement, they would have to learn good and evil to develop in Eden. We may never understand how God planned to implement lessons on good and evil, but they needed knowledge of this, without which they couldn't have made correct choices, govern, and mentally, psychologically, and emotionally mature.

Knowledge is the first step in humanity's mental maturation; it teaches them how to think and make cogent choices. Consequently, conscience, the guiding principle of man in the second dispensation, is based almost exclusively on his ability to decide what is good and what is evil. I do not believe this was God's method of introducing good and evil into the frame of knowledge of humanity, but inevitably, knowledge separates saints from sinners based on their abilities to choose between good and evil. It is a guiding criterion that sets boundaries in every cycle, but beyond that, the greatest of choice is the decision to follow God's will, to choose to be obedient to His will. We must choose to let His will be our guiding principle even in our contentiousness. We must suspend our will and choose to let His be done.

The need for this knowledge surfaced early in the plan of salvation and verifies how significant it was. The ability to decide must underpin our socioemotional and psychological infrastructure; it determines our rationalization abilities and differentiates us from lesser life forms; it maintains a hierarchy in physical creation until we are again indwelled.

I understand why it might have been difficult for Adam and Eve to make appropriate decisions with few options to choose from. Some think it should have been easy, but we must also look at it realistically; they were in a vast world with so little information and knowledge; that spells wrong choices. This is no excuse; it's simply a realistic perspective. Eden must have been a restricted and monitored reserve for Adam and Eve as they grappled with the lessons they had to learn.

The Cycle of Conscience

And she again bare his brother Abel. And Abel was a keeper of sheep, but Cain was a tiller of the ground. And in process of time it came to pass, that Cain brought of the fruit of the ground an offering unto the LORD. And Abel, he also brought of the firstlings of his flock and of the fat thereof. And the LORD had respect unto Abel and to his offering: But unto Cain and to his offering he had not respect. And Cain was very wroth, and his countenance fell. And the LORD said unto Cain, Why art thou wroth? And why is thy countenance fallen? If thou doest well, shalt thou not be accepted? And if thou doest not well, sin lieth at the door. And unto thee shall be his desire, and thou shalt rule over him. (Genesis 4:2–7 KJV)

The cycle of conscience was the period for defining and perhaps developing knowledge of good and evil, right and wrong. Moral is an adjective that relates to the principles of right and wrong and is the process of conforming to a standard of right or wrong behavior.

Here, very early, came the lesson on the acquisition of morality, the doctrine or system of moral conduct. Humanity's actions could then be evaluated ethically. We may use the words *ethics*, *morals*, or *standards* interchangeably, the rule by which a characteristic or caricature can be justly arbitrated. We can certainly see why the Lord built systematically on these modules.

I maintain that Jehovah had planned the extent to which we were required to grow morally good and the necessity for that growth. The Tree of the Knowledge of Good and Evil would be important in the garden only after Adam and Eve had acquired good moral standards. This is a reality check for every sincere child of God; His loving, tender mercies are everywhere evident and are nurturing and facilitating our free will; He is there to guide us in our reasoning. He exemplifies patience for our good, but the refining fire still tests the quality of the ruling element we must come to. Job said, "But when he has tried me, I shall come forth." Well, I think that this statement would be more appreciated in the future; it wasn't so productive for Cain and Abel.

The story of Cain and Abel is very likely the moment when the Lord fully implemented His system of morality. I see this as probable because of the extremely stringent evaluation of the brothers' abilities to choose. The practice of animal sacrifice after God introduced it on Adam's behalf is not indicated in Scripture, and we cannot be sure God established the conditions for such a sacrifice. It is nowhere stated that Adam had to sacrificially appease for his wrongs. It has not been revealed whether Adam was present for the first sacrificial ritual, performed by God, nor can we say he was supposed to teach the procedures of sacrifice to his sons.

First, if Adam was not required to observe animal sacrifice and thus had not taught his sons this, Abel must have heard of it from his parent and thought to offer meat based on moral consciousness. Second, if Adam had taught his boys to offer blood sacrifices, then Cain's action was immorally reprehensible because he chose evil: "And the Lord said unto **Cain**, Why art thou wroth? and why is thy countenance fallen?" (Genesis 4:6 KJV). These questions would have been valid only if Cain had known the options but nonetheless made his choice.

Since the lesson was introduced at the end of cycle of innocence, I think God's questions were not random ranting. He was incapable of asking such questions on the eve of establishing morality without having defining the principles of sacrifice. God is incapable of vain interrogation. His questions indicate that He was asking them from a clear frame of knowledge or expectation and that Cain and Abel knew the choices they had. The rhetorical questions confirm that the choices were clear and available to Cain. God said, "If thou doest well, shalt thou not be accepted? And if thou doest not well, sin lieth at the door. And unto thee shall be his desire, and thou shalt rule over him" (v. 7) Here, God explicitly reminded Cain that choosing to do right was an option.

Even so, I feel God's reprimand of Cain was not condemnatory; it was a prompt. He explained to Cain the severity of making wrong choices. Though Cain's action was not the first sin, it was the first time disobedience was so named by God and the first time sin was mentioned in the Bible. He exposed Cain's mentality to the nature and attitude of sin. God introduced sin as a dangerous, predatory stalker. He told Cain that whenever wrong choices were made, something predacious was pursuing the will. If he had chosen the right sacrifice, it would have been accepted.

Conscience is the nucleus of our ethical psyche, a reference base that begins with a clear knowledge of options and outcomes. Cain's anger was due to his having made the wrong choice that resulted in calamity. He felt that regardless of the decision he had made, the choice had been his to make and it should have been accepted regardless of its moral nature. Unfortunately, many think this way instead of seeing morality as the ultimate check and balance on the psyche.

A difficult situation arose out of this squabble. Cain's anger led to his bitter resentment of his brother, who had had absolutely nothing to do with God's decision. The only possible reason for his spree of misdeeds was his immorality. He became irate because his brother's sacrifice had been accepted, and that created a new sin—jealousy, or at least apparent jealousy. Tests were an essential concept in the growth process; they produced growth. The sin that was hunkered down on his back was a dangerously complicated accomplice of anger. But introducing the negative side of disobedience is essential for growth.

Free will means we can make our own choices, but we still have a responsibility to God to make the right choices. The knowledge of choices is a judicious awareness, an act of self-governance. God created man a free moral agent with a dead soul; the Spirit was not responsible for monitoring his morality. His free will exposed him to the necessity to know right from and wrong. God said that reprisal was a cowering invader. Sin is the consequence of reprimanding.

This second cycle was to teach man morality and ethical growth. God used this period to set up the frame for humans' psyches. This is the censorious link in the sequential development of man primarily because it establishes a platform for his psyche. What man is required to learn here would become principles for centuries of the practical implementation of dominion. There would be an immediate scrutiny of the perimeter of choices in human government as humans were called upon to make judicious decisions. Finally, the breath of God is the infusion of conscience. When Jehovah breathed into the nostril of man, he was spiritually and morally conscious; he was illuminated.

We have already dissected to some extent the consequences of the extinguishing of the breath of God in man. All humans have the capacity for spiritual reasoning, and the essential knowledge that needs to be in place in the third cycle hinges strongly on humanity's understanding of the necessity and the efficacy of veracity.

The Cycle of Arbitrary Introduction

> And God blessed Noah and his sons, and said unto them, Be fruitful, and multiply, and replenish the earth. And the fear of you and the dread of you shall be upon every beast of the earth, and upon every fowl of the air, upon all that moveth upon the earth, and upon all the fishes of the sea; into your hand are they delivered. Every moving thing that liveth shall be meat for you; even as the green herb have I given you all things. But flesh with the life thereof, which is the blood thereof, shall ye not eat. (Genesis 9:1–4 KJV)

Before we begin our study of the major principle in this cycle, let us have a look at the covenantal agreement once more and particularly at the promises God made to Noah. God's promises are sure; because of His guarantees, we have come to expect them. The indemnity of these promises is palpable today. The

Noahic covenant is the covenant of a new beginning; in it, God renewed the Adamic covenant with only subtle changes. Many of the original concepts of the Adamic covenant are viable. Man was told again to multiply and replenish the earth. The literal translation should read, "God looked compassionately upon Noah and his sons and blessed them. Through them He reinstituted the Edenic assignment which he had given Adam, He told them, 'Be fruitful and multiply, replenish the earth.'" This entreaty was in keeping with the mind of God in the process of procreation and found in all the cycles except promise. In Genesis 15:5 KJV, Jehovah promised He would do the multiplication: "Look now toward heaven, and tell the stars, if thou be able to number them: and he said unto him, so shall thy seed be."

There are other embellishments of this mandate in Genesis; the consuming of flesh was one of the defining aggrandizements in the Noahic covenant. Jehovah authorized Noah and his descendants to consume any flesh they desired. With the attached condition, they were not to consume the blood from any of the animals or birds, because it was their soul. The dietary shift might appear mundane, but it was the final setting of human dietary guidelines. Of course there were major adjustments in the cycle of the law but only for the chosen people and for ceremonial rituals.

> And the fear of you and the dread of you shall be upon every beast of the earth, and upon every fowl of the air, upon all that moveth upon the earth, and upon all the fishes of the sea; into your hand are they delivered I have placed them in your power. The animal would fear and dread man, and they were now available for food. (Genesis 9:2 KJV)

Jehovah imposed two more major sanctions on Noah. First, humanity was to maintain a semblance of dominion in the form of a primitive government. This command seems simple, but the mandate that humanity would rule over the animals in fear and dread was a judgment call on our authority to enforce dominion. Think about it; God does nothing in anger. So to say you will rule but only through subordinating in fear is a serious implementation in the contractual agreement with Noah. The hallmark of Jehovah's providence is the graceful presence of encouragement through lovingkindness rather than through hatred and dread, which is not how we are treated. We must team them by forcing changes in their attitudes and if necessary through brute force. Indeed, this is a step out of the way of nurturing; it's closely related to the sentence passed on Adam, which was to subdue by the sweat of his brow.

The third cycle is the era of human government. Again, this name is very relevant to the purpose of cycle. First, it is a new beginning, a time when humanity would exercise a more proficient role in supervising creation. Humanity had been evaluated and elevated. However, Noah kept the covenant of works and Adam's assignment on Noah's return from the ark. He planted a vineyard, but we shall soon see that this generation's obligations were more detailed and complex than just controlling weeds. The devotees of this cycle were to control humanity through moral fortitude.

Second, the promise of the rainbow was our final look at the new addition to covenant adjudication. After the flood, God promised He would never again flood the earth because of evil in humanity's heart. This was the second flooding of the earth by Jehovah because of the disobedience of His creatures. He promised Noah there would be judgments of other nature.

The rainbow is more than a casual reminder of the flood; it was the foundation of a covenant of promise with a preview to building faith and trust. God always established precursors of the governing principles for subsequent dispensation. Here, He planted a nonbinding or obligatory seed of promise; however, its presence was a reminder.

> And I, behold, I establish my covenant with you, and with your seed after you; And with every living creature that is with you, of the fowl, of the cattle, and of every beast of the earth with you; from all that go out of the ark, to every beast of the earth. And I will establish my covenant with you; neither shall all flesh be cut off any more by the waters of a flood; neither shall there anymore be a flood to destroy the earth. (Genesis 9:9–11 KJV)

He blessed His creation and commanded them to be fruitful and multiply and replenish the earth. As with every other cycle, God selected a leader with whom He would establish the covenant's agreements for the cycle. Noah was selected the progenitor of human government with the responsibility of moderating the earth and enforcing the governing principles of the cycle.

In this progression of development, Jehovah sought to establish the first human government, a new system that would lawfully litigate the function of free will and arbitrate humanity's behavior by judging its consciousness. It didn't mean they would become monarchs; it required humans to be accountable for their actions and responsible for their choices. From then on, they had to think about their actions and be solely liable for their choices based on morals and ethics. For any governmental system to arbitrate based on honesty and integrity, it needs a strong ethical and moral platform.

The trial and errors of conscience in the previous cycle were the threads that established such a judicial system's benchmarks. It must literally or inferentially set standards that quality decisions must be possible and definable if justice, impartiality, and fairness were to govern. Ethics must become the principle for mediating right and wrong, honesty and dishonesty, if there were to be equitable decisions.

It might strike you a bit heinous that even after God's spiritual appeal to Cain for submission and repentance, he chose not to heed the warning. We will see a bit further on in these developments and particularly during the age of the Messiah that for God to accommodate humans, they have to have spiritual consciousness. Human government seeks to choreograph humanity's behavior and assuage people's actions.

God permitted the first murderer to live unpunished for the unprovoked homicide of his brother. The institution of human government was established with the notion that justice would be served on lawless and rebellious people. It was meant to restrain heinous evil such as murder and other acts of violence against humanity to mitigate the surging evil that so severely grieved God that He regretted having created humanity.

> And surely your blood of your lives will I require; at the hand of every beast will I require it, and at the hand of man; at the hand of every man's brother will I require the life of man. Whoso sheddeth man's blood, by man shall his blood be shed: for in the image of God made he man. (Genesis 4:5–6 KJV)

A major principle of human government was the establishment of capital punishment for murder. This system would require a human tribunal to investigate murders and apprehend the perpetrators. It's difficult to wrap our thoughts of maturation around this concept, but God instituted capital punishment to deter us from committing atrocious, inhumane actions. It was the new ruling principle added to the agency of dominion or governmental control. Humans were at that point knowledgeable, or should have been, enough to be arbitrators and enforcer of laws; they were growing in their understanding of right and wrong, and they had the knowledge to make decisions about good and evil and define boundaries between punitive or imputative acts. Though we will not hear of names of felonies and misdemeanors until the law, it's believable that a system was in place.

As early as this, we are able to detect the development of a complex system of rules and regulations functioning on morals and ethical standards and outlining the consequences. As far as the progression of dominion is concern, at that point, humanity was then equipped to litigate as a tribunal and thus control a community and humans. This has to be a remarkable stride considering the hypersensitive nature of the progression of humanity's submissive actions to the Creator. It's human nature to control but not be controlled.

The first fully established earthly governing system was a theocratic government with a hierarchy, theocracy being the highest. In a theocracy, earthly leaders are directly advised by God. The later Jewish high court, the Sanhedrin, is an example. Eventually, Israel asked for a human monarchical government as its neighbors had; and God gave them King Saul.

A standing tribunal did not mean a restoration of dominion; it was only a major development in part to the dominion lost to Adam in Eden. These developments were now typical symbols of futuristic reality. Regrettably, the actual beauty of dominion was lost as a consequence of sin; restoration would return only after the salvation of the cross. We will never know if dominion would have reached us through Adam; we know the second Adam's form but not that of the first.

When God brought the animals to Adam to see what he would name them, they obeyed His command cheerfully and out of love. The epitome of dominion at that time was different; in Eden, it was one of bliss enveloped in love and cheerfulness. In the phase of human government, however, the authority of governing was enforced only through fear. This governing principle is so ungodly, but many good but very misdirected Christians think this is how God deals with us daily.

We can see that through these transformations, the Lord's workmanship was being progressively returned to man so he would continue his missed training. He had to submit with an awareness and a conscious knowledge of the effects of his actions on his environment. However, with the knowledge acquired during the past progressions, man was more mentally equipped to manage the works God entrusted him with, but unlike innocence, this required bringing him into submission. Through this, we may glimpse the dominant roles humanity was expected to perform as the caretaker; through these cycles, they developed in this capacity.

The lessons of the past two cycles have certainly added credence to the evolving of man's psyche. He gained new knowledge that bolstered his governing status, but sin remained a source of much distraction.

Man remains alienated from the true source of help and fellowship with his Maker because of his sinful nature; however, he is painstakingly progressing despite his iniquity. The grace of God through the Holy

Spirit is also an influence. Despite these acrimonious debilitations, it is clear that God is still very concerned with our well-being.

The Cycle of Promise

> Now the Lord God had said unto Abram, get the out of thy country, and from thy kindred, and from thy father's house, unto a land that I will shew thee: And I will make of thee a great nation, and I will bless thee, and make thy name great and thou shalt be a blessing. (Genesis 12:1–2 KJV)

The fourth Cycle of human maturity began with the singling out of a devotee who would be God's mediator in the epoch as God had done in the previous periods. This selected individual was a type of the Savior. God designated an intermediary to establish and maintain His presence as He taught and demonstrated His purpose to bring humanity to His mandates for its evolution.

In the dispensation of promise, God chose Abram, a seventy-five-year-old man, and Sarah, his wife, who was sixty-five. I mention their ages because they were the defining quality that validated God's absoluteness. God called Abram out from among his people to use him to establish and reserve a people for Himself. This is not a new beginning as was the Noahic covenant.

God wanted a people He could call His; He wanted a chosen race, a people singled out from among the nation of the earth not just to be called the unique lineage of the Messiah. He did this to establish and maintain a relationship with those who would offer true worship to their Creator and be an example to the rest of humanity. God's care for His people was clearly seen through the historical record of His interactions with them. God's purpose for this is everywhere in the Bible, commencing from the call of Abram to the arrival of the Messiah. Abraham and his descendants were almost exclusively the major subjects from Genesis 10 to Malachi. In that span of time, God used these people to teach and test every developmental growth process He had developed.

In this fourth cycle, faith became a necessity. Ultimately, faith is absolute trust in God; it is being assured that if we trust and believe God, the things we hope for will be guaranteed. Faith is wholehearted and blind trust in God. It has always been a requisite for relationship with God, a deeper purpose intended to develop trust so God may in this theater of development establish providence through faith-based participation.

Receiving from God requires an established faith walk. Faith has always been a part of the maturity efforts, but because of the ruling component contingent on promise, faith in Jehovah became a prerequisite. For man to elevate his status and interests, he had to develop a faith-centered dependency on God. The ultimate promise is not an Isaac but a Jesus.

The second concern of ours is the cancellation of the demand for the multiplication of population despite the earth being only sparsely populated. We will no longer hear the command to multiply and replenish the earth as had been uttered in previous cycles. Jehovah has chosen a people to be His children upon whom He will place the distinction as the children of God; these He has promised that he will grant himself.

The multiplication of the descendants of Abraham is one of this cycle's cardinal promises. Its fulfillment is not covenant; there are no contingencies upon which Abraham's participation was required to make it come to pass. Though the direct command was not explicitly stated, its sentiments were present in one of the major promises to Abram; Jehovah told the patriarch that He would make a great nation out of him. There is only one nation whose population number as the sand on the seashore. This promise is an apocalyptic calculation of the church of the Lord Jesus Christ.

Jehovah wished to make prominent the constituents of faith through these promises. By choosing an old man and a barren woman past childbearing age, God knew it would take a giant leap of faith and an equal stretch of the imagination for them to even think about this. The inception principles set up to implement this promise were designed to eliminate all exterior possibilities of humanity or nature. God did this to build faith by ensuring that the outcome could be attributed only to Him, but the idea was so fantastic that the participants couldn't help but laugh.

We can see this could not be a promise for peopling the earth though there is a mention of a large number of people; Jehovah Himself took on the assignment. The huge number of descendants was intended to show the limitlessness of Jehovah's power. He even took on an infertile woman unequal to the challenge of imagining this. Here, among these people, we will learn about the nature and characters of God and faith among humanity by and through whom humanity would experience Jehovah.

The promise made to Abraham was extended to his children and strangers; the beneficence of His presence was a promise. Although God did not intend to change the structure of the second cause, procreation, He shifted His command for humanity to be fruitful and multiply. He promised a senior couple He would use them to people the earth. This is the main concept of the Abrahamic covenant.

The covenant of promise was based solely on the promises God made to Abram. In Genesis 12:1–3 KJV, God used the phrase "I will" four times. The significance of this clause will become evident in the enactment of the covenant. Abram was put into a deep sleep; he was not a participant when the Lord passed between the sacrifice. Some suggest Abram must have passed between the sacrificial offerings earlier that day, but the first-person narration of the Lord lends strength to the notion that humanity's involvement in this covenant wasn't arbitrary. Faith requires active participation, but it hinges on the idea of following and believing as opposed to actively participating. There could be no credible reason for Abram to become actively engaged in the legalities of the cycle of promise.

In Hebrews 6:13 (KJV), we read, "For when God promise to Abraham, because he could swear by no greater, he swore by himself." A promise is not always an actual contractual agreement; however, its presages what a person is willing to do either on the presuppositions of a covenant or contract between two parties or an unconditional agreement, which would be a non-commitment on the part of one of the participants. Holding a person to a promise is not really good faith. Simply having faith that a person is true to his or her word is grounds enough for resting in expectation.

Faith is a factor in all the cycles. Although the Abrahamic covenant's governing principle was faith, it was not included as a prerequisite for the fulfillment of the promises God made to Abraham. Ironically, the promises were designed to call us to faith. The promises were unconditional to Abraham, but ultimately, their manifestation hinged on obedience. This must be understood so we don't bind the call of Abraham from among His people as a condition to the covenant's promised dependencies. Though it might appear to be the case, God swore to bring these promises to pass. Disobedience and unbelief have always been our greatest sins. The lapse of time and the lack of faith by Abraham and Sarah before the manifestation was a disheartening display of disobedience.

> And it came to pass, that, when the sun went down, and it was dark, behold a smoking furnace, and a burning lamp that passed between those pieces. In the same day the LORD made a covenant with Abram, saying, unto thy seed have I given this land, from the river of Egypt unto the great river, the river Euphrates. (Genesis 15:17–18 KJV)

Some believe the transaction of this covenant came from midlevel Eastern customs. When two or more participants joined in an agreement, they performed exactly the same rituals as Abraham did, or when they did not, they invoked the lamp as their witness, which has been from time immemorial inscribed on the minds of Eastern people. This custom was not a new practice to Abraham. The Lord Himself descended to ratify the covenant. The patriarch did not pass between the sacrificial parts because he was not obligated to contribute anything. He asked for a sign that the compact was sealed, and by passing through the sacrifice alone, Jehovah affirmed that He would keep His promises.

Faith and obedience were the only conditions attached to this arrangement. The first request by God to Abraham was a call to obedience, for him to leave his original country: "Get thee out of thy country, and from thy kindred, and from thy father's house unto a land I will show thee." (Genesis 12:1 KJV) This is a major stipulation to an expectation, however, the familiar phrase 'If thou shall' which seems to be a requisite in many Biblical covenants, to enforce the agreement of the conditions is not enacted, but God did not put any riders in this covenant. The familiar "if you will" that reinforced the arbitrary features were not in force, but I am not suggesting that the subjective phrase "If thou shall" was the lingo of biblical treaties for binding arbitration in a covenant agreement.

We may see the cycle of promise as a contract through which Jehovah personalized His will, which must be accomplished. To enforce His authority, He convened the contractual agreement of this cycle with Himself. The "I wills" mentioned at the onset and that appeared at the beginning of this chapter were guarantees of God's stipulation for the patron of this cycle. These promises were paradigms for strict adherence; they were presented in an ominous theater of impossibility to showcase His authority.

Looking at Sarah drifting toward a hundred years old might create dramatic irony in Abraham's mind. It was almost as if he were saying, "Tell me when to stop." At Lazarus's grave, "Jesus said, Take ye away the stone. Martha, the sister of him that was **dead**, saith unto him, Lord, by this time he stinketh: for he hath been **dead four days**. Jesus saith unto her, Said I not unto thee, that, if thou wouldest believe, thou shouldest see the glory of God? (John 11:39-40 KJV)

It was a call to faith. The apostle Paul said, Sara's first conception was a seed. Before she could give birth to a child, she had to birth a seed. Certainly, incidents like these make it impossible to doubt God. They are binding because it is through these kinds of supernatural manifestations that faith in God's authority is manifested.

> Now the LORD had said unto Abram, Get thee out of thy country, and from thy kindred, and from thy father's house, unto a land that I will shew thee: And I will make of thee a great nation, and I will bless thee, and make thy name great; and thou shalt

be a blessing: And I will bless them that bless thee, and curse him that curseth thee: and in thee shall all families of the earth be blessed. (Genesis 12:1–3 KJV)

The first promises are called major because they contain personal guarantees. The second promises are minor or general promises to curse those who cursed him and to bless Abram's families. You know the saying, "If God said it, it is settled"; that should have been sufficient. Well, that's easier said than done.

God promised Noah that He would never again destroy the earth by flood and that the rainbow was the sign He was monitoring the heavens. However, He made other promises about earth's future. If He had promised a rainbow would appear to remind us that rain would not become a flood, He has upheld that promise. The Bible said God does not lie and the Son of Man had no reason to repent. If He said it, He will bring it to pass. We must not take His promises lightly; we must take the promises of fire or pestilence as equally binding as His promises of prosperity.

The development of the promise cycle is unique. In comparison to the previous dispensations, one of God's prominent interests was the obligation of multiplying and replenishing the earth, but in this cycle, Jehovah promised He would make of Abraham a great nation. What was once a prominent command had been turned into a guarantee.

We may see the rainbow as an incentive to the appeal for faith. It certainly takes a good stretch of faith to believe that God would use rain to remind us not to worry, that earth would not be flooded, but the appearance of a rainbow during a rainstorm can certainly encourage faith.

As we watch the overriding theme take its form in this developmental cycle, it seems that the Lord was purposefully activating a defining proactive faith-based system unlike any He had done before. As the community of man became becomes more and more sophisticated, God used the experiences to set up a system based on consciousness with expectations that had not been seen previously.

Though this system means to expose His continual providence or authority, He wants us to understand that living and moving requires distinguishing trust and belief in Him with clearly stipulated criteria. Saints must understand that boundaries in this case and in all others past and future are set by the level of faith with which we approach God. The Bible says that without faith, it's impossible to please God. This is not new; it has always been the benchmark for entrance into providence. Nowhere has it ever been the exception to the rule, but when we say faith sets the boundaries, we must look to the gospel for the answer to that statement. Jesus told His disciples that if they could only believe, nothing was impossible.

The appeal for faith through promises is a bold and decisive outreach by Jehovah for us to turn from our disobedience and unbelief. The promises of God are His direct outreach to prove He is spiritually and emotionally interested in our welfare, but these promises contain more. They contained the exclusive self-committed obligation of our God for the direct working of His purposeful will on our behalf. This means that man's development will proceed only because of His divine intervention.

It is also a call for the Lord to be in control of our spiritual and emotional development. When we trust and obey Him, we are basically saying, "I choose to believe you and accept your will and direction for my path into development and prosperity." This must be our mind-set because He will have to periodically suspend our agendas not just for our best interests but also so divine providence might take its course.

Jesus taught us that anyone who could produce faith the size of a mustard seed could see mountains removed. As great as our needs might be, this is all that is necessary for us to enter the providential government of God.

This may seem to be a tremendous lowering of the bar, but faith had a niche; it must be blind. "We walk by faith, not by sight," Jehovah said though He had made fantastic, unconditional promises; what was needed to produce the manifestation was a proactive faith. The Scripture informs us that Jehovah stands behind His Word, that His promises are sure! We will see God manifest promissory results when faith is invoked for petitioning.

God will produce manifestations contrary to our disposition to engaging belief systems. Just as He respects our free will and will not arbitrarily override our decisions because He can or allow His will to become indiscreet, He will sometimes suspend our free will and enforce His superiority. There are things He needs to accomplish for the general good of the masses. There are occasions when He is at work in things too subtle, as well as things, too grand to be perceived by man's intellect.

The majority of the Abrahamic promises are self-binding and are contingent solely on Jehovah's benevolent providence; at times, He supersedes human objectives because there are too many developmental tangibles too subtle for our participation.

The intent of the promises is to develop our hope and faith. By them, Abraham could look for a city built by God. God established great and precious promises in that time that cannot be humanly duplicated or accomplished outside His involvement. This is so that His children will come to recognize His endearing presence and will build reliance on Him. Also, they are in part intended to take our minds beyond the edges of humanity and beyond the senses to look to the hills whence cometh our help. This teaches us God's superiority and authority.

A grander trajectory is the reinstitution of fellowship and relationship with Him. He desires a people who will take pride in being called His children and among whom He will be delighted to establish His presence, but still, there is a far superior purpose in this period. His choosing a people established a lineage from which He would bring forth the Messiah. The Savior of the world will come from this chosen people. He will have a lineage that would be traceable back to the inception of this people. There is more to it than just that. Jesus told us that anyone who entered a sheep corral any other way than the door was a thief. This traceable lineage gave God's Messiah historical proof that He was man and could take our place. The gospel record of His lineage shows that it was a highway for His advent. Certainly, the gatekeeper was the Father who sent His Son to be the Sun of Righteousness.

> Verily, verily, I say unto you, He that entereth not by the door into the sheepfold, but climbeth up some other way, the same is a thief and a robber. But he that entereth in by the door is the shepherd of the sheep. To him the porter openeth; and the sheep hear his voice: and he calleth his own sheep by name, and leadeth them out. (John 10:1–3 KJV)

Many things can be accomplished but only when iniquity is eradicated from the mind of humanity. When we use the term His people here, we are speaking generally inclusive of all of mankind, not just the minds of His chosen people but Gentiles as well. In Hosea 1:10 (KJV), He said, "**Ye are** not **my people**, there it shall be said unto them, **Ye are** the sons of the living God." His chosen people were to teach the other nations about the one true God.

> And I will sow her unto me in the earth; and I will have mercy upon her that had not obtained mercy; and I will say to them which were not my people, Thou art my people; and they shall say, Thou art my God. (Hosea 2:23 KJV)

The apostle Paul drew from the book of Hosea to validate the inclusion of all nations; He said in Romans 9:25 (KJV), "I will call them 'my people' who are not my people; and I will call her 'my loved one' who is not my loved one." He was subtly but clearly suggesting that God had intended to bring all humanity together in Christ.

Jehovah meant for all people to have an active role in their maturation, but it is difficult to understand the full purpose of this covenant. It was a contractual agreement between God and humanity in which He established a contractual alliance with a significant individual for a set period. The uncertainty, however, remains whether it was to establish a corporate faith among these people or to hold an individual responsible for the development of the ruling factor in the cycle. For whatever purpose, singling out an individual has been a standard procedure from the beginning of the restoration of humanity since the covenant of works and was the formula up to the Mosaic covenant.

The birth of Isaac was the crowning moment in the promise; the impossible was manifested. Amid the laughter and disbelief of Sarah and her husband, Isaac, the promised seed, arrived; the first of millions was born through which God would corroborate His promises. It took God twenty-five years to get Abraham and Sarah to the place in Him where He could produce the manifestation, but they tried themselves to get to that point.

When the covenant was first confirmed, Sarah was sixty-five and Abraham was seventy-five. Their actions delayed the process. God overrules free will at times, but that is not His general approach in dealing with disobedience. As long as they felt they needed to help God along, God was not going to get involved in the process: "I am the Lord: that is **my** name: and **my glory** will I not give to another, neither **my** praise to graven images" (Isaiah 42:8); but unquestionably, there had to be an absolute understanding that what happened did so through God alone. By delaying the process, He removed human possibilities from the equation. Consequently, twenty-five years had been wasted before this couple finally let go. Only when their efforts failed and their hopes died was God able to accomplish His will.

A ninety-year-old woman gave birth just as God had promised amid laughter and disbelief. God's promises came true after twenty-five years. All the efforts exerted by Abraham and Sarah to help God only demonstrated our inability to trust God.

Ishmael was not God's promised seed. God's promise was not contingent on Abraham's participation in the producing; a man can have children long after a woman cannot. The miraculous manifestation was upon Sarah, who had been created with limited capacity. The fight was mainly realized through her. No wonder she fought to move the process along; for her, the glimmer of hope was fading, but men during Abraham's days were in the prime of their fatherhood years, and the Creator is never anxious. A man may father a child well beyond the years of a woman; but for a woman, menopause means the end. She has produced her last egg, and every woman has only a certain number of them. When that number is depleted, you are done: Menopause.

The apostle Paul said she gave birth to a seed; this could be grounds for deep discussion because women do not have seed. Mary had a seed, but it was planted in her by the Holy Spirit. Perhaps the apostle was using seed and egg interchangeably.

Was Sarah the major agent in this contract? She was mentioned only as a minor contributor, but her role contributed greatly to the promise; God's reasoning was to draw her husband into the contest of faith by retrogressing menopause in his wife. We may question her reaction to it; why did she see it as a nutty trick, something to laugh about or at? But God wants us to know that if we are to live healthy lives, we must understand we have to live beyond what we know and understand. One of the cardinal purposes of the promise is that He created reality from the unseen. This would be a solid foundation on which to build faith. It is confounding, but we cannot deny its manifestation; Isaac was alive and kicking.

Isaac's birth validated the contract and its promises. This event revealed that Jehovah was able to do all He said He would do despite disbelief. Without a firm faith agreement, nothing upon which to stand, Sarah gave birth to Isaac. When we understand the magnitude of God's greatness in this pregnancy, the inception of a virgin birth is conceivable. I'm not suggesting that the birth of the Messiah was contingent on the human capacity to believe Him into existence; what I am suggesting is that faith is a huge experience. The Messiah would erect a kingdom whose governmental infrastructure was not of this world; its entrance is only through faith. He said those who hadn't seen but still believed were blessed.

If you can believe the possibility of the birth of Isaac, you could look with great faith for the arrival of the Messiah. The promise may seem self-furnishing, but it points to the advent of the Savior. God did this to show us two things. First, He wanted to prove His abilities to us through the fulfilling of the promised seed; we were given revelation of His power that was to help us build faith that one day He would send a Savior and to trust Him and rely on Him. Second, it might be a stretch of imagination, but could it also be a preview of the possibility that God would come down and interact with us as Christ to reconcile the world to Himself?

Isaac's birth demonstrated the purpose for God's promises. Though Isaac was his only son, Abraham trusted God and would have sacrificed him. In the fulfillment of the promises was revealed the great principle of a maturing faith. Faith is a necessary agent in the advancement of Christian maturity. We may also realize through the promises that God is not calling for faith as much as He is trying to establish faith-based development. If it were only for faith, Abraham and Sarah would have had a son and would have lived happily ever after.

A faith-based development might be called a corporate faith that would open an eye to the messianic advent. Through faith, the chosen people could then join Abraham in looking for a city whose builder was God. This serves us as the representative of expectations.

Chapter 8

The Dispensation of the Fullness of Time

That in the dispensation of the fullness of times he might gather together in one all things in Christ, both which are in heaven, and which are on earth; even in him: In whom also we have obtained an inheritance, being predestinated according to the purpose of him who worketh all things after the counsel of his own will: That we should be to the praise of his glory, who first trusted in Christ Ephesians 10–12 (KJV)

In these words resonate the greatest notes on the doctrine of salvation though this concept could be enormously challenging to comprehend. The nucleus of the apostle's thought is simply that heaven and earth are united in Christ. We find this idea tough to understand when we think of the configuration and operation of the universe's governance. Even searching ways and means to look at the machinery of heaven is problematic.

The apostle intended to bring together the idea of the terrestrial and the trans-terrestrial unification under one head. The fall of humanity was so catastrophic that it destroyed even the economy of providence. See Genesis 28:12 (KJV), which speaks of a dream Jacob had about a stairway resting on the earth with its top reaching to heaven; angels were ascending and descending it. Above it, the Lord said, "I am the LORD God of Abraham thy father, and the God of Isaac. . .". This vision by Jacob is a glimpse into the machinery of providence. The Greek word for *providence* is *pronoia*—"forethought," "foresight," and "provision for." Providence is the administering and conjecturing care of God. God's providence upholds and governs everything. It is coextensive with the universe and as unceasing. All His attributes are engaged in it. This concept might stir a compelling uneasiness, but sin had created an uncrossable canyon that ended God's providence.

Understanding the universality of Jesus' position in creation would substantiate the possibility of the reinstitution of heaven and earth in Him. To better facilitate our assistance in understanding the restoration of providence, the apostle Paul said in Colossians 1:16 (KJV), "For by him were all things created, that are in heaven, and that are in earth, visible and invisible, whether they be thrones, or dominions, or principalities, or powers: all things were created by him, and for him."

Jesus is Lord of all things; this is the essence of restoration. This union of all things makes available a clear glimpse of the reinstatement process of dominion, but the apostle extended this thought far beyond the concept of the seven-day creation process. It established that creation had been restored to the control of humanity through the man Christ Jesus. We can certainly see the essential necessity for the garment of flesh of the Lord Jesus Christ. It specified and sanctioned His lordship though He is every whit God. Its distinguishing qualities present in him as the second Adam.

Second, the reinstatement included things in heaven and perhaps wherever the jurisdiction of the Ancient of Days extended His prerogatives. Let's try wrapping our minds around the concept of the authority of the God in Christ. It is an arduous request of imagination the apostle Paul summed up very beautifully in 1

Timothy 3:16 (KJV): "And without controversy great is the mystery of godliness: God was manifest in the flesh, justified in the Spirit, seen of angels, preached unto the Gentiles, believed on in the world, received up into glory."

We understand that by so associating with flesh, certain restrictions came about. God's cardinal attributes could not accompany Him. We may understand this through the teaching that He emptied Himself before He took on human flesh though it was not as yet glorified though not fashioned after the similitude as Adam. Upon His resurrection, as the first begotten from the dead, His garment of flesh was glorified although this could not be confirmed as the reasoning behind the qualification for the reinstatement of His authority.

He told us in Revelation that He had taken back the keys of death, hell, and the grave. This statement of victory confirmed that the enemy was no longer the god of this world. For before the glorification of the body, in Him dwelled the fullness of the Godhead bodily, and so the Pauline mystery persists. To this, the Lord declared all power in heaven and on earth was His. He took back Satan's power and added to that the power in heaven and earth.

This may seem incomprehensible, but if Christ is our life, our life is hidden with God in Him far above all principalities and powers. It is the essential structure of the fulfillment of the cycles of maturation. We are complete in Christ Jesus. Colossians 1:16 (KJV) places a handle on the idea of this teaching by the apostle.

> For by Him all things were created, both in the heavens and on earth, visible and invisible, whether thrones or dominions or rulers or authorities—all things have been created through Him and for Him. He is before all things, and in Him all things hold together. Colossians 1:16 (KJV)

This Scripture is in harmony with John 1:1 (KJV), but the Pauline doctrine raised the person and character of Christ to a distinctively exclusive position in the counsel of God. This revelation reveals the pre-incarnation authority of Christ.

In the gospel of John, we learn all things were made by Him. We recognize even in this teaching a conception of a transcending of the idea of creation in Genesis. It points to an all-inclusive summary of the creation of God, but scholars suggest that John's account of Creation generally addressed the Genesis version exclusively. The magnificence of the revelation is too grand to elaborate intelligently, so it appears as if to deal with it, it was handled triflingly. I believe that because of the magnitude of the expanse of the revelation and its direct connection to the Christ, it has become much too disproportionate because of dogmas. The person and work of Jesus Christ have been reduced to our reasoning abilities.

The apostle Paul taught us that the creative work of the Lord was inclusive because it superseded the Genesis concept. Our difficulty in comprehending this extended knowledge of creation arose when Paul explained specific concepts of the creation: All things visible in heaven, certainly this knowledge transcends our ratiocination, for it includes the administration of God and the total angelic host. (Colossians 1:16) Through Paul's disclosure, we must understand that we are no longer addressing only the creation works of Genesis that describe Creation; just as this requires a stretch of the analysis to process, Paul said that in the dispensation of fullness of time, God placed everything under the control of the Son.

The dispensation of the fullness of time is equally a phenomenon; it brings together in one all creation, not just Jews and Gentiles. There is a popular notion that suggests that angels cannot engage in redemption activities, but this hugely popular idea must be revisited! The angels who lost their estate and were reserved in chains of darkness are being held until this ingathering. I am not suggesting their salvation, nor am I suggesting they can be saved, but they were created by and for Christ. One certain thing is that the repositioning of the creation includes them. "That in the dispensation of the fullness of times he might gather together in one all things in Christ, both which are in heaven, and which are on earth; even in him."

In this time, the Father gathers all things in Christ, Hallelujah! Creation's intention has been repaired to make known the intention of the Adamic covenant. Just as Christ is every whit man and God, we can be every whit man and God. We can be partakers of human and divine natures simultaneously. The foundation for God's likeness and image has been reinstituted. The possibility of becoming copartners with Christ and sitting with God in heavenly places in him has been made available again through the awesome sacrifice of Christ.

I use the word *can* liberally because all things can be restored through the Savior. The fall of man and the birth of sin have stained creation and have opened an unbridgeable gorge from the fall to the advent of the Messiah. The crucified one is a bridge over that canyon. One of the great sayings of the gospel is in Luke 2:14 (KJV): "Glory to God in the highest, and on earth peace, good will toward men."

The gist of the angelic message is overlooked because of its association with the birth of the Savior and not what the Savior brought. This heavenly manifestation had nothing so much to do with the birth of the Lord as with the purpose of His coming. Not many other statements in the gospel are as cogent as this. It heralded the glad tidings that the time for God and humanity to be reconciled had come. Reconcile in its literal definition means reuniting, bringing together again. This bringing together was not two individuals reuniting in fellowship and friendship. No! In this reconciliation of oneness, man would be reconciled to the image in which he had been made.

Second, reconciliation is an all-inclusive function of the atonement of the Lord Jesus Christ. God was in Christ reuniting humanity and Himself. He relit the spirit of humanity that would fuel the growth of supernatural life.

For the earnest expectation of the creature
waiteth for the manifestation of the sons of

God. For the creature was made subject to vanity, not willingly, but by reason of him who hath subjected the same in hope, Because the creature itself also shall be delivered from the bondage of corruption into the glorious liberty of the children of God. For we know that the whole creation groaneth and travaileth in pain together until now. And not only they, but ourselves also, which have the firstfruits of the Spirit. (Romans 8:19 KJV)

The atonement of our Lord and Savior Jesus Christ paid that heavy toll for sin. Sin had inflicted a devastating toll on creation that was so devastating that nature itself couldn't escape spiritual death. Christ was the sacrificial Lamb on which God laid the iniquity of us all. He who knew no sin became sin so that we might become the righteousness of God in Christ Jesus. The death of Christ was the toll that was exacted for the possibility of relighting the inner lamp. "He was wounded for our transgressions, he was bruised for our iniquities: the chastisement of our peace was upon him: and with his stripes we are healed."

But he was wounded for our transgressions,
he was bruised for our iniquities: the
chastisement of our peace was upon him;
and with his stripes we are healed. All
we like sheep have gone astray; we have
turned everyone to his own way; and the
LORD hath laid on him the iniquity of us
all. (Isaiah 53:5–6 KJV)

Romans chapter eight echoes the great sentiments of this glad narrative. On behalf of those who want to ask the question, but dare not, I will assume the audacity to act on their behalf and ask the question. Why do we find it impossible to comprehend Jesus Christ? We take away His humanity and demand He act like God. This is a terrible mistake. Jesus didn't come to act like God, nor did He. He was the man Christ Jesus. Who really is Jesus? The answer is simple: we may want part Savior from heaven and part Savior from mental manufacturing, but He did not do his messianic work as God, not even His miracles.

To begin to make sense of this ever-expanding acquisition of knowledge of the Lord as He reveals it to me, I am committed to grasping this knowledge that has exceeded all my literal and spiritual education. He is indeed God who alone is past finding out! We were able to clearly distinguish the presence of a Savior in all the cycles of maturation though not as a forceful as the experiences of the atonement, but nonetheless, the types and theophanies were understood as pointers to a deliverer.

In all the cycles of maturation, the concept of the Messiah was revealed; however, some of these manifestations were in the form of difficult theophanies and were manifested in many forms. Many were revealed in association with environmental occasions. These manifestations came to culmination in the fullness of time in the incarnation. In the personification of the Lord Jesus, God was in Christ in the fullness of the Godhead.

The presence of a savior was made known in every cycle. In the first cycle, the Messiah was the Word and the Word was God. In the second cycle, He was the sacrificial offering. In the third cycle, He was the ark that preserved Noah and his family. In the fourth cycle, He was the ram caught in the thicket. In the fifth cycle, He was the Pascal Lamb, the blood on the posts of doors, the tabernacle, manner, and the captain of the army of God. In the sixth cycle, He was God in man. In the seventh cycle, He was the Alpha and Omega.

Old things are passed away, and all things become new. All things are of God, who hath reconciled us to himself by Jesus Christ, and hath given to us the ministry of reconciliation; To wit, that God was in Christ, reconciling the world unto himself. (Corinthians 5:17–19 KJV)

God was in Christ. In the fullness of time, He emptied Himself and took on the form of a servant. The great job of the servant Savior was the reconciliation of the world to God, who was in Him and through Him overseeing this great resolution.

The great mystery of God in Christ in the flesh may well be beyond the purview of the human comprehension, but Christ had to be man to be the Savior. For in the creation the only authority of stewardship over the creation was consigned to humanity, which was created and authorized to communicate with God. So in the process of reconciliation, it had to be humanity actively assuming the role in the reuniting process. First, God is all powerful and does not need the conformation of dominion. He gave that role to humanity, so humanity must secure the position. But the creative authority belongs to the Creator. The Word had to become flesh. In Genesis, God spoke the Word and the Spirit moved. The personification had to contain the Word, the creative force, so it became flesh, and at His baptism, the Word was again empowered by the Spirit to create a new generation. God gave the Spirit to Him without measure.

> For by him were all things created, that are in heaven, and that are in earth, visible and invisible, whether they be thrones, or dominions, or principalities, or powers all things were created by him, and for him: And he is before all things, and by him all things consist. (Colossians 1:16–17 KJV)

The work of the Word in the flesh is reunification. The Genesis life force that had been snuffed out by the fall was reinvigorated by Christ the life giver. Jehovah was in Christ reconciling the world to Himself. He did not take back the authority. We have touched on this subject a little earlier when we tried to understand how dominion would have worked through Adam. But all things are His! Colossians 3:3 (KJV) tells us, "For ye are dead, and your life is hid with Christ in God. When

Christ, who is our life, shall appear, then shall ye also appear with him in glory."

Scripture does not reveal how the power source of dominion would have worked through Adam. But in grace our lives are hidden with God in Christ, who is our life. He affirmed that all the Father has is His and all that is His is ours. So reunification is not an attempt to monitor the power but to make sure nothing will ever again separate us from the love of God.

All things were created through Him and for Him. This is the sophistication of the authority of God. The restoration of things are held together and kept in check in Christ, who is reserved in heaven to be revealed at some time in the future. Because He lives, we shall also live.

In the dispensation of the fullness of time, the Father reconnected all things through the Son. Let's look at the restoration of humanity, which was liberated from the bondage of sin through Jesus' blood. Our ability to choose has been reinstated. We can once more become a part of the divine nature if we choose. We can do all things through Christ, who strengthens us. We are one; control is in our hands, for at the name of Jesus, every knee will bow.

The genesis life force is once more an accessible option. Jesus said, "If anyone come to me out of his loins will flow rivers of living water." Christ is our life force. He restores us to the Father. "If any man be in Christ, he is a new creation, old things have passed away."

Chapter 9

The Lord Jesus Christ

> Till we all come in the unity of the faith,
> and of the knowledge of the Son of God,
> unto a perfect man, unto the measure of
> the stature of the fullness of Christ:
> That we henceforth be no more children,
> tossed to and fro, and carried about with
> every wind of doctrine, by the sleight of
> men, and cunning craftiness, whereby
> they lie in wait to deceive; But speaking
> the truth in love, may grow up into him in
> all things, which is the head, even Christ.
> Ephesians 4:13-15 (KJV)

The gospel serves two major purposes: to build faith in Jesus Christ, and to point the way to reach maturity in Him. The two ideas are so closely related in their purposes that at times it is difficult to differentiate between them. Since these two principles or paradigms are the general unanimity of major Bible studies, it would be best to treat them as separate studies.

Paul informed the Ephesians in chapter 4 that the gifts of the Spirit were for the edifying of the church until it came into the unity of the faith and knowledge of the Son of man unto a perfect man. It is worthy of note that building faith does not necessarily equate growth in and of itself. The Lord said, "Those who know better and choose not to do better, will be beaten with many stripes"; there is a difference between knowing and growing. Growing is becoming: "When I was a child, I thought and acted as a child, but when I became a man I put away childish things." (1 Corinthians 13:11)

These two ideas under discussion are being scrutinized because both have the same trajectories: knowledge of Jesus Christ. Let's combine the two ideas under the theme of knowledge, for both are defined by the same terms. A converging of these ideas will better suit our analysis of faith because the Christian faith is built up through the knowledge of Jesus Christ and maturity is spiritual development through this knowledge; one seems to be an end to the other. However, to be able to fully understand Christ, a fully developed faith-based system structured through a careful study of Christology in the cycles is fundamental to our ability to understand Christ. Our choice of studies will track four messianic concepts in the cycles. We will begin at their latency and end at their maturity.

A good course of study should include topics such as the Anointed One, the sacrificial symbolism of the atonement, theophany, and the indwelling and typology among many others, this list is not all inclusive by no means. This knowledge would serve for us as the base from which to study the messianic concept as a methodical historical concept emerging out of primitiveness. It underpins three major theories in this work

First, these concepts are structured to validate that cycles of developments were carefully crafted to be established through a growth time. Our Creator had established actions to buttress the growth of salvation. In these cycles, He had not left anything up to chance. Nothing was at the whim of evolving into something meaningful or meaningless; there was no detour of ventures.

Chapter 10

The Anointing

> But you shall receive power when the Holy
> Spirit comes on you and you will be my
> witness in Jerusalem, and in Judea and
> Samaria and to the ends of the earth. Acts
> 1:8 (KJV)

The subject of the anointing is hotly debated in Christianity. There are many variations of the theory of the anointing, suppositions real and imaginative from the nature to the purpose of the anointing.

The word *anoint* in Greek is *chrio* and in Hebrew *masah*; it has been used many times in Scripture. The derivative *anointing*, in Greek *charisma* and in Hebrew *hagion*, which refers to specially prepared anointing oil, is found thirty-nine times in the Bible, but *charisma* is the only form in which it has appeared in the cycle of grace. In the gospel, *charisma* is not merely a figurative name for the Spirit; in his first epistle in 2:26–27 (KJV), the apostle John wrote,

> But you have an anointing from the Holy One, and all of you know the truth. But the anointing which ye have received of him abideth in you, and ye need not that any man teach you: but as the same anointing teacheth you of all things, and is truth, and is no lie, and even as it hath taught you. 1John 2:26-27 (KJV)

Here, the word signified that an anointing was a communication with and a reception of the Spirit. *Charisma* refers to the presence of the Spirit not particularly as a state of being but as a function of the Spirit.

> Howbeit when he, the Spirit of truth, is come, he will guide you into all truth: for he shall not speak of himself; but whatsoever he shall hear, that shall he speak: and he will shew you things to come. (John 16:13 KJV)

In John 16 (KJV), the function of the Spirit, *echete*, means "Ye have an unction" and in verse 20, "Ye have received." In this gospel, the anointing serves as a reminder of our calling in Christ. This passage introduces preinstruction to the arrival of the Spirit and therefore should address the presence of the Spirit, not the anointing. When the apostle wrote, "He will guide you into all truth," he was referring to a help, unction, to act of the Spirit: "But ye have an unction from the Holy One, and ye know all things" (1 John 2:20 KJV).

The word *anointing* is used interchangeably with the word *unction*, which appears only twice in the gospel. The Greek form of the word for anointing is *charisma*, unction. This form of the word is used in the 1 John 2, where it refers to the act of unction, to the empowering act of the Holy Spirit. Jesus encouraged His disciples to wait in Jerusalem until they received power.

In the Law and the prophets, the Hebrew term for the word *anoint, masah,* is extended to the word *mashaiach*, which means "Anointed One to be," which is close to *chrio* and its sacred derivative *Christos*, "the Anointed One," the Messiah. In this form, *anoint* has appeared numerous times in previous cycles to grace. The Hebrew mashaiach has multiple definitions. First, it is associated with the anointing of people chosen by God for prominent assignment. David received mashaiach from Samuel the prophet; David was the one Jehovah had chosen to replace Saul.

First, a clear distinction can be drawn between *anoint* in the previous cycles and the *anointing* in the cycle of grace. This form of anointing is not directly associated the gift of the anointing by the Holy Spirit, charisma, but with the appointment of kings, priests, and other notable assignments from God as we have already made clear.

This term "Anointed One," Christos, also applies to the Messiah as an attribute of the Christ and appears especially strong when used in the prophetic sense to the rise of the Davidic throne and the expectancy of the coming Davidic ruler who would sit on the throne of his father, David, as the Anointed One of Israel.

The anointing or charisma in the cycle of grace is significantly different; it is an efficacious agency of the Holy Spirit, the presence and authority of the power of God in the new creation. It is the power of the indwelling presence of God. Know this: your bodies are the temples of the living God. This effectual agent serves as the authority responsible for changes and for help in destroying opposition to the changes.

The anointing is decidedly diversified and highly effective, able "to do exceedingly and abundantly beyond all we can think or imagine." It is the enabling help that Jesus had promised would come and work alongside us until the rapture of His church. As we strive to embrace the divine will of God for our lives and take on the divine nature, we are facilitated by the gift of anointing.

At the new birth, every Christian is anointed. Being born again literally means an infusion of the Spirit of God and the anointing. We must carefully draw this distinction between the Holy Spirit and the anointing of the Spirit. First, the Holy Spirit is the third person of the Trinity; the anointing of the Spirit is an agency of His, the effectual nature of the Spirit.

Christ, the light of the world, lights the lamp of God, which is the soul of us all. This is the act of being born from above. As many as received Him, to them He gave the power to become the children of God. However insignificant this new life might appear, it is a miracle. God reconnected through the Spirit to perform the transformation from the kingdom of darkness to the kingdom of light with one of His. From that point on, we commence our journey of embryonic sanctification into perfection, until He sees Himself in us.

For he whom God hath sent speaketh the words of God: for God giveth not the Spirit by measure unto him. The Father loveth the Son, and hath given all things into his hand. (John 3:34–35 KJV)

The Spirit of the Lord is on me, because he has anointed me to proclaim good news to the poor. He has sent me to proclaim freedom for the prisoners and recovery of sight for the blind, to set the oppressed free, to proclaim the year of the Lord's favor. (Luke 4:18–19 KJV)

On this particular Sabbath in the temple, Jesus took the scroll, something He was accustomed to doing, and read from it. This is indeed a worthy note, for many are under the erroneous teaching that Jesus lived in Arabia up to this time. However, on this occasion, He read from Isaiah 61 KJV.

The spirit of the Lord God is upon me; because The Lord had anointed me to preach good tidings unto the meek; he hath sent me to bind up the brokenhearted, to proclaim liberty to the captives, an the opening of the prison to them that are bound To proclaim the acceptable year of the lord and the day of vengeance of our God; to comfort all that mourn. (Isaiah 61:1–2 KJV)

The focus here was on the revelation of the necessity of the anointing; even Jesus Christ, the Messiah, had to be anointed. We have already agreed that the anointing is the presence of God's power through the Spirit, which cannot be conceived in a womb. God was not and could not be born of a woman, but the man, Christ Jesus, had to be born of a woman to be every whit man. The gift of the anointing was delivered directly from heaven. John the Baptist said, "I was informed that upon whom I see the Spirit descending, that person was the Lamb of God which takes away the sins of the world." God anointed Jesus with the Holy Spirit. He did not receive the Spirit without measure because He was a perfect man though one above the law of man and nature, a perfect being. He received the Spirit as mediator and author of salvation; in Acts 10:38 (KJV), we read how God anointed Jesus with the Holy Spirit and power. John 3:34 (KJV) tells us,

"For the one whom God has sent speaks the words of God, for God gives the Spirit without limit."

Christ is the manifestation of all types and archetypes of the Anointed One. Israel's anointed priests and nobles were only shadows of the Lord. Though it was essential to establish a traceable lineage for the Messiah, He preceded the Davidic lineage. He is the author and the finisher of our faith. All Christians are gifted with the anointing with which our Lord was gifted.

The anointing emboldens the saints to become more productive in actively opposing the work of the enemy. This is the chief reason the disciples were advised to remain in Jerusalem before they commenced their ministries. Jesus informed them that they had to wait for the Spirit, who would empower them. This was spiritual equipment.

On the day of Pentecost, Peter stood up under the anointing. After a soul-stirring sermon, old argumentative Peter, now transformed, spoke with such intellectual competence from the unction that five thousand souls were born into the church as a result of that one sermon. With the strictest confidence in the power of the anointing of the Holy Spirit, Peter and John were so thoroughly convinced that all that was needed was to tell the crippled man, "Take up your bed and walk" and he would. The phrase "got up leaping and jumping" eliminates any doubt about the power of the anointing.

Jesus demanded that His disciples remain in Jerusalem for this very essential empowerment from on high. Setting off in ministry without the help of anointing will always be disastrous. In the case of the eleven, the Spirit had not yet arrived, and they needed its power in creation's new reality.

The anointing destroys the yoke of the Adamic nature. Some believe that the deformed appendages of the serpent were vestiges of legs before he was cursed to slither along the ground for the rest of his life. Just as conscience or any other agency of maturation begins in latency, the anointing of the Spirit in us commences embryonically. No, we do not become born again today and start casting out devils immediately.

> And John answered him, saying, Master, we saw one casting out devils in thy name, and he followeth not us: and we forbad him, because he followeth not us. But Jesus said, Forbid him not: for there is no man which shall do a miracle in my name,

that can lightly speak evil of me. (Mark 9:38–39 KJV)

What the Lord said was that this man had reached a level of maturity in spirit and that his faith had grown to a functioning level; he was well on his way to the image and likeness of Christ. Demons are not responsive to mimics, but a firm faith can move mountains.

Sanctification is the process of dying daily to sin and growing daily in grace and the anointing of God into His divine nature. In the short quote above, Jesus was speaking about the quality of a matured growth. Anyone who had reached a level of the anointing and faith to be able to cast out demons could not overnight descend to the level of blaspheming His name. This level is the result of the process of systemic growth and cannot be immediately eroded. There is no malfunctioning of the anointing.

The anointing is a multifunctional operation of the Spirit that helps us reach beyond our human potentials. It is transmitted to us and supervised by the Holy Spirit, for spiritually empowering the new creation. Its major function is to empower us to preach the gospel to every nation and tongue. We are to be his witness to preach the Gospel to man, "until they all come into the unity of the faith, unto the knowledge of the Son of God, unto a perfect man." It makes us able to produce in ourselves a working manifestation of the likeness and image of God.

This unique help from God facilitates our reasoning abilities and enables the saints to rationalize in the God conscientiousness. This consciousness is our ability to be led by the Spirit in determining what is right and wrong in pursuit of God's perfect will. The power to speak, to claim, to forgive, even the power to love are all influenced by the anointing.

We need help to love some of the people we encounter daily. Through the Spirit, we can love even our vilest enemy and bless those who treat us spitefully and scandalize our names. The development of love is a true sign we are spiritually growing.

He bolsters us to go into the throne room of God boldly and make our petitions. The Bible teaches that those who speak in unknown tongues edify themselves. It is a form of spiritual communication manifested only during elevation in the power of the anointing. It is an inner communication, a way of talking to God that is unintelligible to others.

The anointing is also present to assist us in our everyday needs. Its major purpose has already been introduced, but it also helps us communicate with others. Jesus assured us that there was no need to worry about what we would say when opposed by powerful authorities, that the anointing would speak through us.

I spent many hours writing this book to share with you what God wanted you to know. There is no way I could have written this book without having an intimate encounter with the Spirit. Prayerfully, He will give you feedback and clarity on the new information you have encountered. This is precisely what edifying the body means.

You may already know a great deal about this, but taking a glimpse at one or two pages will jolt your memory of the wonderful time you have spent with the Lord studying and a particular lesson you received some time ago. When Jesus said, "We have no need on anyone to teach us, because the Holy Spirit is our teacher," He meant teaching like philosophies, the devising of heretical concepts and paradigms based on deducing dogmatic conclusions. The apostle Paul added some clarity to this complicated subject.

> From whom the whole body fitly joined together and compacted by that which

every joint supplieth, according to the effectual working in the measure of every part maketh increase of the body onto the edifying of itself in love. (Ephesians 4:16 KJV)

Some people have taken this statement by Jesus to literally mean never read any book other than the Bible, but we are required by the Spirit to edify one another. The anointing structures a mental guide along this line that directs and redirects the thinking process. The Lord lets us know it's not our responsibility to contend with what to say. The Spirit will bring all information to our conscious mind at the appropriate time and enlighten our mental or spiritual direction through revelations.

One of the great beauties and wonderful treasures in the anointing is that it sometimes hedges us in during confrontation. Some think of this hedge as some kind of a spiritual barrier for our protection. Soldiers have to stay calm in extreme circumstances. The anointing from the Holy Spirit hedges our conscience, Hallelujah! If we hold our peace, He will fight our battles. Think about a difficult encounter you've had but minus the pressure that accompanied it. St. Paul addressed these likely struggles, calling them conflicts of the journey.

> We are troubled on every side, yet not distressed; we are perplexed, but not in despair. Persecuted but not forsaken; cast down, but not destroyed. Always bearing about in the body the dying of the Lord Jesus, that the life also of Jesus might be made manifest in our bodies. (2 Corinthians 4:8–10 KJV)

At times, we face issues that are too complicated to comprehend or cope with; the anointing is our source of strength gifted us to live supernatural lives in a natural world. "I can do all things through Christ who strengthens me." This supernatural influence that empowers us to preach the gospel is the essence of that great treasure we have in earthen vessels. This is glad tidings for the poor, and it will restore people to normal living, proclaim freedom to the captives, open blinded eyes, set people free of demons, and empower us for transitioning into His divine nature. This is all possible only through the anointing of the Holy Spirit.

But the manifestation of the Spirit is given to every man to profit withal. For to one is given by the Spirit the word of wisdom; to another the word of knowledge by the same Spirit; To another faith by the same Spirit; to another the gifts of healing by the same Spirit; To another the working of miracles; to another prophecy; to another discerning of spirits; to another divers kinds of tongues; to another the interpretation of tongues. (1 Corinthians 12:7–11 KJV)

We receive personal benefits through the anointing. Besides the enabling by the Spirit for edifying the church, the Holy Spirit enhances the personal gifts and talents of those who dedicate themselves to the glory of God. Although I believe all gifts and talents are covered under the gifts of the Spirit, I don't believe gifts and talents are intended for personal use; people abuse their God-given talents.

Now there are diversities of gifts, but the same Spirit. And there are differences of administration, but the same lord. And there are diversities of operations, but it

is the same God which worketh all in all.
(1 Corinthians 12:4–7 KJV)

Performing artists are notorious for abusing their gifts. I recently heard a cut of an old hymn sung by one of the heartthrobs of the seventies, an R&B artist who brought his audience to their feet in praise to God. Was the praise of these worshipers real? Perhaps. Was he real? Not in my opinion; not for what he had come to fame for singing, but the Word is still good in hellish mouths.

God's words are eternally anointed spirits empowered by the anointing; they are the wisdom and reasoning of God and will not return void. This is obvious based on numerous incidents in Scriptures in which God used people even in strategic roles. This is true even in the lives of many of our contemporary gospel superstars; God anoints the lyrics for His purpose. I've even seen artists using mimicking gestures very effectively in place of the anointing to trigger emotional responses.

Just as there are many manifestations of genuine anointing, there are many manifestations of palliative anointing. The differences in the anointing vary from denomination to denomination; some denominations make outrageous claims about the manifestation of God's power. The snake wranglers claim they have been anointed by the Spirit to pick up poisonous snakes safely. Such cults have misunderstood what "You will take up serpents and they will not bite you" meant. These literalists devise damnable dogmas because of poor biblical understanding and the idea the Bible should be taken literally. Tragically, they claim the anointing will protect them from the poisonous beasts resulting in unnecessary fatalities.

Some preachers teach the outrageous heresy that the anointing is gifted in three levels. Listen: as you transition from a corrupt nature to a Spirit-filled nature, the power source shifts and your faith and conscience shift. As you grow in the grace of God, you will think, believe, and act more like Him. His Word is His wisdom. The level of the anointing depends seriously on the level of your maturity. As you grow and become more like Him and your functions mature, your spiritual growth creates a greater capacity of the anointing. The new power is not bestowed; it grows into what it is to become. The more you become like Him, the more you think like Him, the more confident you will be about yourself and the more faith you will have in God at work in you; no wave of a magic wand.

One popular evangelist claimed he had visited the tomb of a saint known to have been mightily used by God in signs and wonders in the gospel ministry. He claimed his body shook from the anointing coming from her tomb. He alleged he could feel her anointing. Think seriously for a minute here; the Bible encourages us "to work while it is day for the night comes when no one can work." At death, the Bible says, "Absent from this body, we are present with the Lord." You do not get a do-over.

There are no distinguishing levels to the anointing. As we die daily to sin, we grow daily in His divine nature. The born-again saint is a unique, new creation. We must become children, and that requires a complex repositioning of our souls' functions. Everything must return to its Edenic potential. The nature of the old man must die daily as the new man acquires the knowledge of Jesus Christ of life eternal. "Till we all come into the unity of the faith, and of the knowledge of the Son of God, to a perfect man, to the measure of the statue of the fullness of Christ" (Ephesians 4:14 KJV).

The fruits of the Spirit are the common characteristics of Christlikeness; they are all part of God's divine nature. For example, when we become peace or love, we grow in His likeness and image. Jesus became flesh; He came in our likeness and image to take on sin and die in our stead so we might have everlasting life. The more we are drawn to the likeness of God, the more the presence of God increases in us, hence the greater the manifestation of the anointing. Speaking of the fruits of the Spirit, the apostle Paul said, "Against such there is no law." The more we become like the Lord, the more authority we will have to act on His behalf even contrary to nature.

As many as received Him, He gave them the power to become His children. We are born again as babes in Christ with full potential; however, the babe has a fresh start but is spiritually infantile. We are all anointed as children of God, but to get closer to Him, we must die to the world and grow in grace till Christ is formed in us: "My little children, of whom I travail in birth again until Christ be formed in you" (Galatians 4:19 KJV).

The anointing is God's gift that helps the saints of God become partakers of His divine nature. We must keep in mind that all things were created by Him and for Him, and without Him were not anything that was made. Snake handlers and an anointed corpse border on insanity; these ideas don't cut the mustard. These extreme heresies cannot glorify God, and they are extremely detrimental to the integrity of the gospel and its purpose; they cannot administer edification to the body of Christ. Their actions are not palliatives; they are deceptions. Jesus said, "You will receive power to be my witness." The anointing is the inspirational breath of the Spirit.

The word *charisma* doesn't appear in this form in the Law and the prophets or any of the previous cycles because humanity didn't have the capacity for anointing. Now that our souls and spirits, the lamps of the Lord, can be relit, we can become temples of the living God. As we mature and become more like Him, our spiritual growth will create a greater capacity for the anointing; our new power is not bestowed, it grows incrementally into what it is. As we become more Christlike, we will be more confident in ourselves and the more faith we will have in the God at work in us. We will become dynamic forces in the kingdom of God. It is not with a wave of a magic wand; our levels of anointing depend on the level of our spiritual maturity.

Chapter 11

Maturity and the Perfect Man

When we try to understand spiritual maturity as it relates to the fullness of time, we are awestruck by its dependency on the resurrection of our Lord and Savior. Christ had to be obedient to death to be glorified. The plan of salvation balances on the truth of the resurrection. We are at once inundated with an immense number of types and antitypes, of avenues, ways, and highways of information that flow to completion in Christ, the estuary of all things.

When I think of the fullness of time, I imagine a tender sapling planted after the winter thaw and dependent on the warmth and the blessing of April showers to grow and descent its roots into the earth. This is necessary if it is to stand a chance against summer's scorching heat. It has to push out flowers in time and under the right conditions to produce seeds for the fall harvest. The fullness of time is a reminder that the Creator has declared all things ready and in place for the completion of salvation.

The growth stages of our maturity can be likened to a garden plan. The process of our maturation is like that of a tender plant struggling against the forces of nature that are essential to its well-being and maturity. Paul addressed the Romans: "Love not the world nor the things in the world, if any man love the world the love of the Father is not in him!" (1 John 2:15 KJV) As humans, we draw on tangible resources for our daily living just as plants need sustenance to survive nature's brutal elements and forces. They must learn to take what they need to reach maturity. "For we wrestle not against flesh and blood, but against principalities, against powers, against the rulers of the darkness of this world, against spiritual wickedness in high places" (Ephesians 6:12 KJV).

Paul used the development stages of a child as an analogy of the fullness of time: "When I was a child, I acted as a child, but when I became a man I put away childish things." There is an embellishment of this idea by the apostle found in 1 Corinthians 13:10 (KJV): "But when that which is perfect is come, then that which is in part shall be done away."

This analogy works well in defining the nature of maturity primarily because it is progressive in structure. Paul framed his thought commencing in its infancy and then guided the thinking process of his readers until it matured completely. This analogy is emblematic of the whole creation order, which started embryonically but was guided by the Creator and had its maturity realized in Christ, the source of everything. Just as Jesus had to come in infancy and grow, every process of grace is a new beginning that must begin embryonically.

In this lesson, it is apparent that the apostle was also making references to the difference between the law and grace. Many of the types in the law are embellishments of earlier introductions. The types introduced under law may have had their beginning elsewhere, but the apostle was suggesting they were in part embryonic because God rehashed their nature and purpose in the Law. The apostle recognized them as detached, deformed shadows that preceded the images. Their shadows in the law were intended to track to their beginning. They were manifested types in the cycle of grace.

The cycle of grace is the age of maturity, the time of the perfection of all things. This developmental preparedness awaits the completion of the ruling principles in the cycles of human advancement. All governing factors advance from their embryonic stages to readiness and culminate in grace: innocence, conscience, human government, promise, and the law, with all their primitive contributions, are ready and await the Anointed One. We have tracked the five major governing factors from their inception through their various stages of development from their cycles or dispensations.

In Genesis 3:21 (KJV), we read, "Unto Adam also and to his wife did the LORD God make coats of skins, and clothed them." The idea of a dying Lamb of God supersedes all other efforts in place for the redemption of humanity. This idea began its shadowy journey and took shape through the rituals of animal sacrifice, the first of which was performed by God. This first sacrificial offering performed in Genesis, is the earliest introduction of blood sacrifice which would typify the messianic atonement. The fall of Adam and Eve rendered them naked, consequentially there arose the necessity a blood sacrifice. This nakedness here represent multiple entrance and requires explanation. I will go with the idea that the soul emptied of its life force or the breath of God is dead; the depravity of all the honor, joy, and security of their paradise estate is a fitting representation of nakedness.

They contrived the idea of sewing leaves together to cover themselves. This thought will require a closer look; but the general gist of the idea is that this is the birth of sin and leaves could never cover alienation from God. It would take a whole lot more than leaves to bridge the canyon sin had excavated. The fall exposed humans to all the miseries and horrors of a spiritually deprived nature devoid of God and subject to His justice. Without the shedding of blood, there is no remission of sin.

But God did not allow Adam and Eve to leave Eden as frightened, spiritually destitute, unclothed outcasts; He clothed them in the skins of animals. This is a lovely glimpse of grace and mercy offered by God at the end of innocence and is emblematic of the Christ's shedding of blood for the remission of all sin.

The ram Abraham used as a substitute for Isaac was an embellishment of this first saving act of grace. It represents the atonement substitute work of Christ. It a type of Christ, our eternal substitute. The substitutive ram in the bush is a major development in the incremental revelation of the Messianic matriculation. It is a major ruling principle, in that it prefigures the substitutery work of Christ. The ram was God's sacrificial surrogate for Isaac. God made Him who had no sin to be sin for us so that in Him we might become the righteousness of God. The Paschal Lamb was another aspect of the atonement intended to draw us in even deeper than the substitute ram. There are a number of implications pointing directly at the restorative procedure of salvation: "For scarcely for a righteous man will one die: yet peradventure for a good man some would even dare to die. But God commendeth his love toward us, in that, while we were yet sinners, Christ died for us" (Romans 5:7–8 KJV).

The power assigned to the blood of the Lamb was the supernatural presence of God's providential healing. The Paschal lamb's blood on the doorposts protected all inside from the angel of death, and this offering was more representative of the crucified Lord. Unlike with the ram, Jehovah detailed the preparation of the paschal offering in line with many concepts of the messianic crucifixion of the Lord, whose blood obliterated the spiritual death of those covered by it.

The blood of the Lamb is God's agency of purification: "Though your sins be like scarlet his blood can wash them as white as snow." (Isaiah 1:18 KJV) Without the shedding of blood, there is no remission of sin. The sacrificial blood delivered the children of Israel but also strangers in their houses; Paul said, [14] For he is our peace, who hath made both one, and hath broken down the middle wall of partition between us; Having abolished in his flesh the enmity, even the law of commandments contained in ordinances; for to make in himself of twain one new man, so making peace." (Ephesians 2:14-15 KJV)

The temple sacrifices in their respective places were not really different from everyday sacrifices; they foreshadowed the atonement, especially the blood poured onto the mercy seat by the priests. This ritual is especially dominant in Jewish as well as Christian literature; it signaled the atonement for sin. All the Levitical sacrifices have enhanced the messianic expectation.

Another clear indication of the readiness of the world for the arrival of our Lord was the sophistication of the Roman Empire. Even the oppressive Roman monarch Herod was troubled at the chattering about the Anointed One, but it was not just gibberish; wise men had been guided by a star to the Anointed One; they wanted to see the one born King of the Jews: "We saw His star in the east and came to worship Him." (Matthew 2:2 KJV)

The greatest promise was that a suffering Savior would come: "He was wounded for our transgression He was bruised for our iniquity and the chastisement was upon Him and with his stripes we are healed" (Isaiah 53:5 KJV). The sacrificial course of the Paschal atonement was a refined theme of types and antitypes that most understood.

The Jewish religion was in all aspect fully developed and ready. The dispensation of the Law had established a heightened presence of consciousness. One of the chief purposes of the Law was the unfolding of sin consciousness and the inability to reverse the condition without the Messiah. Without the law, I was alive, but when the law came, I died. The law was the final development of the knowledge of consciousness; nothing was left to figuring out a course of action to remediation. All the laws and commandments were completely dissected and studied intricately. Jewish scholars had completed volumes on the implementation and practices of the law.

In Romans 7:7 (KJV), we read, ""What shall we say then? Is the law sin? God forbid. Nay, I had not known sin, but by the law: for I had not known lust, except the law had said, Thou shalt not covet." Though we were first made aware of the interconnectedness of sin and morality during the cycle of conscience, the schoolmaster, the law, taught with vividness the moral structure of everyday living. We can certainly agree that the directives for choice and agreed-upon principles were firmly established protocols mainly because of the strict teachings of the scribes and even the Pharisees.

"If thou doest well, shalt thou not be accepted? And if thou doest not well, sin lieth at the door. And unto thee shall be his desire, and thou shalt rule over him" (Genesis 4:7 KJV). Conscience is the most critical component in its infrastructure of maturity, and it was completely operational at the dawn of the fullness of time. The ability to make morally binding choices is the objective of salvation. Some will refute this claim, but humanity's fall left no recourse but to raise the place of conscience to prominence and importance. At the close of the cycle of conscience, we see the demoralizing result of immorality resulting from the conscientious evil resolutions of humans' will to choose: "And GOD saw that the wickedness of man was great in the earth, and that every imagination of the thoughts of his heart was only evil continually" (Genesis 6:5 KJV).

Conscience is that principal dynamic most closely related to free will and the blessed gift of being created a free moral agent. Noah, who got drunk and for whatever reason cursed his descendants showed the consequences of neglecting this. This principle is also a huge factor in the cycle of promise. We must always be aware of the role conscience plays in choosing to believe.

Abraham, who should have had admonished Sarah for suggesting Hagar become her surrogate, availed himself of the opportunity. Everyone seems to be content with Sarah being the fall guy and take the blame for her husband's indecisiveness, but Sarah had much more to doubt than her husband did.

Even before the Law was introduced, whether it was an everyday practice or not, at that epoch in the development of salvation, humanity had the knowledge to make serious moral decisions. This is clear from their ingenious strategies to circumvent interpretations of the law to suit their benefits. Attempts to interpret the Law indicate that humanity was spiritually and morally equipped to accept or reject the Messiah.

The development of a world governing system was another indication that the road to the Messiah was fully developed. The negotiation to erect the tower of Babel might have been a primitive endeavor, but it was evidence of a governmental structure. Of course, many governmental bodies were in existence then and others were created in many cultures, but nowhere was it more defined than in the great dynasties that led to the incomparable Roman dynasty that dominated world affairs before and during the advent of the Messiah.

The Sanhedrin, the first official religious government, was established for the control of the children of Israel's affairs in the desert under the canopy of the Egyptian empire.

> And they said, Go to, let us build us a city and a tower, whose top may reach unto heaven; and let us make us a name, lest we be scattered abroad upon the face of the whole earth. And the LORD came down to see the city and the tower, which the children of men build. (Genesis 11:4–5 KJV)

After the Exodus and the establishment of a Hebrew Canaan, the formation of a governing body was extremely necessary. Israel's first government was a theocracy ruled by God. It evolved into three different forms of government: the judges, the prophets, and finally their long-desired monarchical system.

After the death of Israel's' military leader, Joshua, Moses' trusted assistant, the judges began their rule over Israel. Othniel, the son of Kenaz, Caleb's younger brother, became the first of eighteen judges, and he ruled for forty years. The rule of the judges ended with the prophet Samuel, who anointed Israel's first monarch, Saul. God called David "A man after God's own heart!" David was the youngest son of Jesse; God anointed him to become Israel's second monarch and vowed the scepter would not pass from his house until the Messiah, the true, Anointed One of whom David was a type would come.

Israel's monarchy came to a dramatic, tragic halt. God warned Israel that an earthly king would be corrupt, that he would use them as his slaves. Unfortunately, this didn't convince the Israelites to change their minds. They not only rejected the Messiah; they also rejected Jehovah. They chose to serve idols; consequently, they were captured by other nations and taken into exile. Their iniquities separated them from their God. Finally, to end the debacle, God stopped communication with them; the silence echoed hollowly for four hundred and thirty years. When the Messiah was ready, when the fullness of time came, Israel was not ready. It was under the oppressive rule of the Roman government, but its governmental systems had been well established.

The cycle of promise, which exceeds conscience, had its roots in the cycle of innocence, but at that time, it was perhaps only an ambiguous, latent paradigm. But its growth persevered and matured in the age of the fullness of time.

Jehovah undertook a tremendous struggle to convince Abraham and Sarah they would be parents and establish the Savior's bloodline, but this was difficult for them to grasp and believe. Nothing was grander than the promise of a Savior who would liberate humanity from sin. The sacrifice of Isaac was a paradigm of this greater promise: If Abraham would sacrifice his only son, God can give His only son. This is the chief promise in the cycle of promise. The choosing of a people and the promises to Abraham were the avenues by which the Messiah, the Seed of Abraham, would come: "For verily he took not on him the nature of angels; but he took on him the seed of Abraham." (Hebrews 2:16 KJV).

Even the monarch of Rome was persuaded that the time of the Anointed One, the promised Davidic ruler according to Hebrew Scripture, was expected. I am curious to know who or what sounded the alarm in Herod's head; perhaps he has spies taking the temperature of the Jewish communities.

Every essential components of groundwork was in place. Rome may have been a tyrannical oppressor of Israel, but it was more than just autocratic; it was the nursery prepared for the gospel. Pilate may have washed his hands, but God creates vessels of honor and dishonor from the same fabric. Rome was an indispensable vehicle for the promulgation of the gospel; it was the most prepared place on earth for the launching of the messianic ministry. The old proverb was right: all roads at that time led to Rome. During that era, more than two-thirds of the civilized world was made up of provinces or vassals of the Roman Empire. All business, commerce, and cultural transactions were handled with Latin and Roman currency.

Greek was the national language spoken at this time, though Hebrews spoke mainly Aramaic, the Lord's vernacular, but it was spoken only as the household dialect; official communications were conducted in the national language. The four gospels and the epistles were written later in Greek.

The law is the fifth cycle in the maturation process; its placement makes it even more significant. Its governing principles, which include all the Levitical laws and the Ten Commandments, encompassed all previous ruling principles; it was a compilation of the types in the Bible. This is not to say that the previous cycles reached their terminations in the law, but the law was the final push, a show of ceremonial conscience.

The elements of the law are recognized as symbolic shadows of the reality of grace. When major references are made of the law in grace, they seem to fall under two very noteworthy concepts: a schoolmaster and a shadow. Interestingly, both concepts signal the incompleteness and the incapability of the law. These two deficiencies surfaced in the inability of the law to make its comers perfect. Paul was most persuasive in pointing out that the law could not produce perfection. This was not a subjective rejection of the law; the apostle meant there was no spiritual nature in the law. He did not mean to undermine or criticize the value of the Law; he meant to point out that the law had run its course. "For the law having a shadow of good things to come, and not the very image of the thing, can never with those sacrifices which they offered year by year continually make the comers thereunto perfect" (Hebrews 10:1 KJV).

In his presentation of the law in Hebrews, he established the concept of the law as a representational shadow, an expectation. One of the main messages in his teaching to the dispersed Jews in this epistle was that the law was only a shadow of things to come. Christ was the fulfillment of the law or the manifestation of types and antitypes.

Let's take up this message and consider the nature of the law and why it was referred to as a shadow. Paul used the Greek word *skia*, "shadow" in Colossians it refers to "something fallacious to the minds but with no substantial manifestation; to epitomize indistinctly or imprecisely." This definition suggests that although the law may have offered moral qualities, they weren't reflections of the more realistic image. The presentation of spiritual qualities was only a presentiment of what was to come. The Law was a shadow having the promise of good things to come. *Shadow* here could mean only crude representations devoid of realization. They had no real substance; they were an obscured, crude reflection of that which was transient and ephemeral. The things representing the person, office, and grace of Christ, the priests for example, were only types of Him; the place in which they ministered was an exemplar of heaven, and the things with which they ministered were but shadows of good things manifested by Christ. Christ was not a priest after the order of the Aaronic priesthood; He was a priest after the order of Melchizedek.

The apostle ended this liturgy with "but the body is of Christ." The body of Christ is the image upon which the shadow of the law draws it imagery, but it can reveal only distorted, transient shadows. Christ is the reality, not a representation of the types. He is the end of types and antitypes. Christ's body represents all spiritual and heavenly things, which have their manifestation through Him.

Paul suggested that the shadows, though only crude representations, were of good things to come but were distorted, rudimentary representations, not replicas of the real thing. The word *image* bears the closest depiction to authenticity, so Paul's usage of *shadow* was intended only to represent a replica. We must conclude that since the nature of the good things to come was the body of Christ, the law could not have been used as a representative of the image of Christ and no comparison to it could be drawn. The sacrifices offered year after year could not make the comers perfect. Through dim obscurity, they pointed to the Messiah.

All sacrificial types are exemplifications of works to be perfected in the body of Christ. Yom Kippur, for example, the holiest day on the Jewish calendar, is observed by Jews as a day of reconciliation or atonement between people and God. It is when Jews endeavored to make recompense to others to draw closer to God. "For on that day shall the priest make an atonement for you, to cleanse you, that ye may be clean from all your sins before the LORD" (Leviticus 10:30 KJV).

When we examine the rituals of Yom Kippur, we see shadows of the two great principles that were to be realized in the gospel: the remission of sin and reconciliation with God. They commenced with the first animal sacrifice in the cycle of works. The Law is a recapitulation of prior studies. The Levitical rituals are nothing more than the shadows of the personalities and operations of Christ. Yom Kippur is only emblematic of the atonement of Christ, in which the Lord was Priest and High Priest and the sacrificial offering for the atonement.

The two goats prescribed as the sacrificial offering for the Day of Atonement prefigured Christ, our atoning substitute. The slain goat was a type of our Lord dying as a sin offering for us. The scapegoat typified Christ rising from the dead for our justification. But the work of the atonement was not completed until the priest put the blood on the head of the goat and drove it into a desolate land. Christ is our sin offering, the Lamb of God who takes away the sins of the world. He who knew no sin became sin on our behalf. He said to Mary, "Touch me not," indicating the assignment was near completion but not finished. "**Touch me not**; for I am **not** yet ascended to my Father: but go to my brethren, and say unto them, I ascend unto my Father, and your Father; and to my God, and your God." (John 20:17 KJV)

Many hold that the ascension the Lord briefly mentioned was a direct reference to the transportation of the blood onto the mercy seat in heaven, but this belief faces contradiction. When Jesus died, the veil in the temple was ripped in half; that signaled the end of the earthly Holy of Holies. I believe due to the exposure and vacating of the Holy of Holies, the actual most holy place received the blood.

Here in the atonement ritual, we see the Lord's two great sacrificial duties: to bring humanity to Christ and to free us from sin. When we inflict our souls with godly sorrow in true repentance and in solemn appreciation of His sacrificial offering, we are saved. The word describes this as a new and living way open for us through the living blood of Christ.

Knowing that a man is not justified by the works of the law, but by the faith of Jesus Christ, even we have believed in Jesus Christ, that we might be justified by the faith of Christ, and not by the works of the law: for by the works of the law shall no flesh be justified. (Galatians 2:16 KJV)

In the second hypothesis, the apostle drew upon the idea that the Law was only the schoolmaster. He is the only writer to apply this sense to the Law, and he used this word three times in Scriptures to reinforce the idea. It was used twice in Galatians 3 and once in the epistle to the Romans. The word in Greek is *paidagogos*, a trainer of boys, a tutor. The English form of the word is pedagogue, originally, a slave whose duty it was to conduct a child to and from school. Instruction was never the primary responsibility of pedagogues; they acted to keep the children out of trouble or self-indulgence.

The pedagogue's assignment was the principle function of the law: to restrain, rebuke, and point out sin. Among the many duties of the pedagogue, to chaperone was chief and especially to chaperone the children to and from school, where they would meet someone who was qualified to properly instruct the children. Paul means in this usage that the law was a schoolmaster to point men to Christ the teacher.

24. Wherefore the law was our school-master to bring us unto Christ, that we might be justified by faith. 25.But after that faith is come, we are no longer under a schoolmaster. Galatians 3:24 KJV

The Law carried out the responsibility of the pedagogue, which was according to the English original meaning, to lead those under the law to Jesus.

First, the Law shows us our sins and its punishments and the incurring danger to the perpetrators. Secondly, the primary purpose of the law was to introduce the comer to Christ. The practical developmental nature of the law solidifies the notion that it could not be a unique entity in and of itself, but rather, it was only a mean to an end in the preparatory progression.

Hebrew 7:18-19 (KJV) "For there is verily a disannulling of the commandment going before for the weakness and un-profitableness thereof. For the law made nothing perfect, but the bringing in of a better hope did; by the which we draw nigh unto God."

Is the law unrighteous? God forbid! To everything under the heaven there is a time and a purpose. Through this we may say that the time of the law was completed. St. Paul said, "The Law was set aside because it was weak and unprofitable." The strength of this verse is mostly obscured because of the direction the lesson took as a result of its interpretation.

By the time Messiah arrived on the scene, the Jews had already built and fortified a culture around the law. There were scholars who were translating and interpreting the law for a living. They may have missed the concepts of its ruling principles, but the law was not cancelled for this. It was completed. Its only purpose was to bring the children to the teacher. Paul writes. "For there is truly a cancellation of the commandment going before for the weakness and un-profitableness thereof"; but we have already discussed, to some extent, the expectation of the law, it was not the image, but only a distorted likeness, a shadow, particularly typical of something else. It was never intended to produce perfection.

The job of the pedagogue is never to school the children. The pedagogue is only a conductor, a tutor. I believe that v19 is a restatement of v18 and was supposed to supply additional information. This thought seems to reiterate in the fact that not only was the law incapable of perfecting the comer, but nothing about it was perfect.

The law which prescribed the ordinance of the Levitical priesthood, by strict ritualistic observances, also demonstrated through these rituals the feebleness of the priests themselves, showing them to be weak, dying mortals, not able to save themselves, much less the souls of those who came year by year; but simultaneously, it pointed to a better hope. The law left the conscience of man guilty. It could identify sin, but it was weak in that it could not expiate sin. There is now a better foundation of hope, a truer path for an entrance into the divine fellowship. Christ is the mediator of a more excellent way.

For Christ is the end of the law for righteousness to every on that believeth. Romans 10:4 (KJV)

St. Paul writes in Romans 10:4, "that Christ is the end of the law..." This statement is much simpler and more-straightforward, than to say, the law was cancelled because it was weak and unproductive. The abled-minded scholar knows that the law is a mean and not an end. It had served its purpose to completion. It could not make righteous, but Christ is the righteousness to all that believe. On that great day of the feast, the Lord stood up in the temple and proclaimed that anyone that come to Him out of their belly will flow rivers of living water. This verified the lesson by St. John, who declares that in Jesus was light and the light was the life of man. In Proverbs 20:7 (KJV), we read, "the soul of man is the lamp of God." We have already had a few in-depth looks at this lesson, but we must introduce it again to confirm that Christ is that Light that soul kindler. It is the infusion of this life from Christ alone that reinvigorates the onset of the New Creation.

> *Therefore if any man be in Christ, he is a new creation: old things are passed away; behold, all things are become new.*
> *2 Corinthians 5:17 (KJV)*

The Word of God says, "If any man be in Christ, he is a new creation, old things are passed away." The meaning of the word creature here, applied in the same manner as used by the Apostle St. Paul when he employed the word, creation, in Galatians

6:15 (KJV). The word rendered "creature" Greek. *(Ktisis)* means properly creation. The act of creating. The essential of the new creation is the reinvigoration of the old nature. The infusing of new life, with its new capacity for moral consciousness, and spiritual fellowship best defines the expression, "new man," found in the Epistle to the Ephesians 4:24 (KJV). The descriptive rendering of the nature of the new man, in this epistle, by the apostle is intended to shed new light on man's personality after conversion. Here, the apostle describes the characteristics of the new man as being created after God in true righteousness and true holiness.

To be in Christ expresses much more enormousness than just a faith ascendancy. Jesus said, "I am the vine ye are the branches. This idea goes much further than just a likeness or an image, this suggests oneness. The oneness in life. There is only one life force, intensity of spiritual maturity determines the degree of manifestation of zoe. The branch and the vine are nurtured from the same source. They have the same physical and mental structures, the same sap supports their growth. When a vine matures, it pushes out branches of extension of its self. This idea presents a more realistic meaning of the statement, in

St Johns Gospel chapter 15 and verse 4, where the Lord said, "Abide in me, and I in you. As the branch cannot bear fruit of itself, except it abide in the vine; no more can ye, except ye abide in me."

Again, to be in Christ, designates likeness and image. All the essentials of the new creation, even our strength is derived from him. Christ is our life. At new birth we are baptized into his fullness, sharing in his blessedness and glory, as the branch receives the same strength and vitality of the parent vine. Anyone who is in Christ, is like him in all characteristic although yet embryonic. St. Paul said, "But I see another law in my member warring after the laws of my mind." I raise this statement to assist in letting the convert know the old nature is not completely eliminated at new birth. So when we say that he is complete in all characteristic of Christ but are therein latent latency, what is being intimate is as many as received Him to them he gives the power to become the Son of God. A new baby has all the potential to be a strong human being like its parents. Eventually, they will learn to walk and talk, but for the present, they can only roll from side to side and make funny gurgling noises.

The relighting of the soul of man is not metaphorical. The re-lighting of the soul of man is a spiritual miracle, it is the reestablishment of the inner man of the heart. His rekindling produces spiritual reanimation. It typifies the on-start of the Edenic life process; but this time, it is through the God-man, Christ the Lord, Himself, the second Adam. The New creation is the establishment of the embryonic image and likeness of God in man. He is a new creation, a new Adam, in a new kingdom.

The old things are passed away behold all things are become new. The old things referred to are the devastations uncured at the fall, the exacted penalties for sin, which were a direct consequence of the Adam's failure. We may define such things as: his heathenism philosophies, bestial nature, his chiliastic rituals and reveries and his earthen standards are all caricatures of his nature. All these consequences are potentially can be removed as a result of the atonement. The arrival of the anointed one is the end of the incubatory age. We are required now to make conscientious choices of whose lordship will rule our lives. Jesus said, "behold I stand at the door and knock if anyone hear my voice and open I will come and sup with him"

Christ is the end of the spiritual evolutionary groundwork. All necessary preparations for the reception and accommodation of the messianic advent was ready. We have discussed to some extent, the necessary preparedness that must precede the arrival of the Messiah. The advent of the Messiah ushered in the advent of the fullness of time. He said, "I am the way the truth and the life, all the laws and the prophet spoke of me." All that came before me were thieves and robbers.

> *My Little children, of whom I travail in birth again until Christ be formed in you. Galatians 4:19 (KJV)*

I agree that the introduction to this verse is debonair and tender, in his writing, St. Paul referred to the Galatians as 'My little children. It shows a tender side of the apostle, he does not find in his labor the deed for suppression. He seemed to recognize that his work was a labor of love. Again, he wrote my little children among whom I travail until Christ be formed in you. Yes, the apostle has a tender side for his audience. Although, he recognized the adversities of his struggle, he does not bring them to bear as the authority to enforce coercion. There are, however, other ways of looking at this remark, it could also mean exactly what it says 'Children'. Newly converted Christians are referred to as babes in Christ. However the tone of the rest of the statement indicates the apostle is not particularly speaking about conversion. He ends the verse by saying until Christ be formed in you. Formation in this usage can also be a synonym of latency, but the formation of Christ does not come at conversion. Although the preaching of the Gospel both saved us, and through it we develop the formation of Christ in our hearts. The difference between these two functions is unique, the latter formation in this case is a synonym of sanctification. Sanctification is the day by day process of dying to the world. We can see an overture of maturity in this declaration. The Apostle distinguished the idea that maturity and perfection is one and the same end in the Christian growth. He taught that the law was unprofitable because it could not make the worshipers perfect. Christ is the end of the law. He has established ministries that are vehicles for the various forms of the presentation of the Gospel.

Ephesians 4:12-13 (KJV): For the perfecting of the saints, for the work of the ministry, for the edifying of the body of Christ: "Till we all come in the unity of the faith, and of the knowledge of the Son of God, unto a perfect man, unto the measure of the stature of the fullness of Christ."

The fivefold ministries of the Spirit is to bring us to maturity. Some have misunderstood the beginning of verse 13. The general perception is that it should be understood to mean, "Till we all arrive at the unity of the faith"; but this cannot be the apostle's intended end, for he has never mentioned the expectation of a corporate maturity. I feel a better presentation of this thought would be, "A full grasp of that faith by each and all of us is the main objective of the ministries of the gifts of the Spirit. Some scholars believe it should say since by and through it both the individual perfection and the corporate unity will be secured. The knowledge that the Apostle refers to in these two verses are the proposition of this work. A knowledge that does not include Church traditions and denominational doctrines. If we are to reach maturity and perfection, we must remove the dogmatic, or hypothesis man has deduced from the course of salvation. This is their empathetic attempt to analyze God. Sometimes they sacrilegiously divert the knowledge to flow in the direction they choose, but if we are to see Christ for who He is, we must come to Him through that unadulterated saving faith that is made perfect by the guidance of the Spirit.

Pure faith makes perfection possible. St. Paul writes, "… and of the knowledge of the Son of God, to a perfect man (that is, full-grown). Earlier we spoke of an analogy used by the Apostle to show the growth requirement of the saints. He said, "When I was a child, I spake as a child, I understood as a child, I thought as a child: but when I became a man, I put away childish things." Here, his idea of a man's development is figurative of the perfect man. See Ephesians 4:13 (KJV)

The chief ministry of the Gospel of Jesus Christ is for the saving of souls and the building of faith by the elucidatory knowledge of the Son of God. Faith alone in Jesus Christ gives salvation. More, there can be no true conversion without the knowledge of the life and work of the Savior. The comer must confess with his mouth and believe in his heart the Lord Jesus Christ, that God had raised him from the dead. Without the resurrection there is no justification.

The second most important duty of the Gospel is to imprint the image of Christ in the soul. This formation of the image of Christ, is the reestablishment of the lost image and likeness of the first Adam. Christ in the heart is the absolute perfect restoration of our divine nature. This impression or carbon copy is the approval of our elevation from brute status to sonship. The new image may not be perfectly humanity, but it is perfectly Godlike, showing forth the nature of God. St Paul ends this thought by suggesting that, *"the measure of the statue of the fullness of Christ."* The measure here refers to the fullness of the Lord, the God in Christ. In him dwelt all the fullness of the Godhead bodily. We, by faith through His atonement, may rightly and justly become a partaker of his divine nature. We shall be full grown men in Christ, attaining to the measure gifted us.

Perfection is completion. First, it is the state of being restored to Godlikeness possibilities. Secondly, perfection means the creation of a new man in Christ has begun; and finally, perfection means the creation of one new man. Christ destroyed the middle wall of partition. This middle wall or partition was the separation and distinction of a chosen people that would show forth the praises and glory of Jehovah in worship. St. Paul declares that that middle wall is now removed. To this end, he asserts, consequentially, there is neither Jew, nor gentile. The new man, who was created after Christ, has no sentiments of dichotomy. The ultimate goal of salvation is to make twain one new man by the preaching of the Gospel. The Gospel brings all people through the seed of Abraham to one new man.

The plan of Salvation or Redemption of man, was the direct and immediate implementation of rescue after the collapse of innocence in Eden. Did God know man would fall? Certainly! Was this salvation a predestinated plan? Although God did not create man to sin, one thing is certain He knew that they would sin and as a consequence would need a redemptive plan of salvation. This plan was introduced in Genesis chapter three.

> *And I will put enmity between thee and the woman, and between thy seed and her seed; it shall bruise thy head, and thou shall bruise his heel. Genesis 3:15 (KJV)*

In this very brief final summarization of the plan of salvation, we are presented a simple, but conspicuous recapitulation of the outline of salvation. God uses the word enmity to basically summarize the movement of salvation. God said, "*I will put enmity between thee and the woman, and between thy seed and her seed.*" The inclusion of the word enmity seems parenthetical to the text. Chiefly because this word is not found in Hebraic language. It is extremely difficult to place this word into this original setting in Genesis. However, the original Latin for enmity is *inimicitatem*, which means "hostile feeling" sets the tone for what is to transpire in the course of the interactions of salvation. The word enmity (n) in its' original form is derived from old French root. In this original form "*inimicus*," it means, "a deep-seated hatred: hostility." In both languages, we find the tracking of the same tone. However, the original old French form of the word *inimicus* seems to be more accommodating in bearing out the mutual sentiments in the indictment by Jehovah, and the ferocity of Satan's' assault. The veracity of the encounter is not a mere stand of, it is a much-related component of salvation. The modern French form of the word enmity '*inimit*', the state or feeling of being actively opposed to someone or something, makes placing this word difficult. *Inimit* the modern French replicates the intended point of view of the writer of this text. It is closest to the design and intention of salvation. This definition is more accommodating in bearing out the sentimentalities of the Creator's purpose in salvation, which is actively opposing the forces of evil and eventually cancelling the handwriting that was contained in the curse on man. What is sobering about the fall is the fact that there is no suggestion that consequentially, God changed His schedule to coincide with the tragedy Adam and Eve were now locked in. The text simply rehearsed what seems to be the usual procedure, or perhaps the intended track.

Genesis 3:8 (KJV) And they heard the voice of the Lord walking in the garden in the cool of the day: and Adam and his wife hid themselves from the presence of the Lord God amongst the trees of the garden.

When the Lord spoke, he did not address the family first, instead, Jehovah's first rebuke and ruling was directed to the serpent. In verse 14, taken at face value, God's first reprimand appeared to be a two-fold directive targeting the serpent. The beast was abhorrent for its action and cursed to a loathsome life; but it is clear from the contents of the rebuke that Jehovah is addressing more than just the beast, otherwise, we are left to believe that the serpent was more intelligent than man. The hostility is to Satan, who orchestrated the attack using the serpent. The futuristic interaction of the devil and the seed is a preview of the conflict that will assail human consciousness. The seed reference by Jehovah is a first glimpse of the redemptive plan of salvation. The Creator's symbolic use of the word seed, prefigures the latency of salvation. Certainly, it also brings to mind the process of development. Jesus said as long as a seed remains in the silo, it is useless, but if it is planted it will yield a harvest.

The seed reference raised two very significant thoughts about salvation that all true believers must understand clearly. In the first ideas, the seeds, 'Thy seed and the woman seed' are archetypal of the conflicts in salvation. The seed also typifies the Lord Jesus Christ, who is the redeemer and the establishment of a new creation of men. This is also the meaning of the seed in reference to the seed of Abraham of which Paul, the apostle, spoke of in his epistle to the Hebrews.

In the second concept, the seed under the heel is a representative of Satan's control and represents all the wicked men who will spring up from all over the world, those who find pleasure in evil deeds, being born in sin and shaped in iniquity. These are the wicked men who will find pleasure in divisiveness. The enemy of the people of God. They are not demons or fallen angels as some supposed. Those Angels are reserved in chains of darkness, they are still awaiting their punishment. The seed of the woman is emblematic of Christ who is the second Adam, which prefigures the Church that will rise in the cycle of grace and become actively engaged in opposing the workers of iniquities.

The second Adam is the anointed one, or Messiah. "Thou shall bruise his heel," the heel does not bear any specific reference to a type, it is the part of the body upon which we walk and is the first to come into contact with the slithering beast. The heel might be a reference to the humanity of Christ, humbling himself in human form as he walks upon the earth. By permission, the devil uses many diversities of tactics to vex and afflict the saints. Jesus reminds us that in this world we would face many trials and tribulations. He said he will sustain our courage by sending the Comforter. So although the devil's intention is negative, what he intends for bad God uses it for our good, God will work the situation for our betterment. Job declared that he had confidence that after his trials, he shall come forth as gold. There is a further reminder by the apostle Paul, in the tenth verse that the end result of trials and vexation of the saints produces the manifestation of the life of Jesus in our bodies.

2 Corinthians 4:8 (KJV): We are troubled on every side, yet not distressed; we are perplexed, but not in despair; Persecuted, but not forsaken, cast down, but not destroyed 10. Always bearing about in the body the dying of the Lord Jesus that the life also of Jesus might be made manifest in our bodies.

The heel bruises the head of the beast, our adversary. The venom sacks of the serpent is in his head. The thought of a bruised-head serpent is extremely provocative. It conjures up mysteries of its legendary fierceness and un-predictableness. The life of the serpent is the head. Decapitate the serpent, but afterwards you will need to kill the head and even then it is dangerous.

A bruised head, no wonder why the devil is typified as a roaring lion, he is inexorable. There is no fatal stroke to this enemy, however, maiming the head of the beast, its principal feature, would impede its defenses and temper his mischief, thus reducing the effectiveness of its ability to strike. This is the enmity that resides between the Church and the forces of darkness.

This crude depiction of salvation certainly carries a clear sentiment of enmity. The development of knowledge is significant in the setting down of evil. Jehovah in His infinite mercies and great intelligence, reveals that people are destroyed for a lack of knowledge. Study to show yourself approved unto God a workman needing not to be ashamed but rightly dividing the word of truth.

Epilogue

There was a time in my early Christian walk when I was spiritually suicidal. I use this term, not to mean losing my Christianity. I was on a quest for Jesus in places where He was not, and I was picking up bizarre rituals to satisfy my spiritual longing; I was thirsty but drinking toxic information. That was the result of not being certain of what to do next. I was called the "praying preacher" by renowned preachers, not just a prayer warrior, but many requested that I pray at their church functions. Lamentably, I recall those glory days as beating the air mostly.

I had developed a rich scriptural reference base. I had committed more Scripture to memory than most, yet I found myself sinking into depression. Fighting off spiritual boredom is a monstrous task. It is depressing when your only spiritual thrill is another new preacher hawking the same old grandiloquence.

Paul said, "Be not only hearers of the word, If a man hears the word and does not do what it says, he deceives his own soul, be not only hearers of the word but doers." Let the Word of God dwell richly on the inside until Christ is formed in us. It's not enough for us to aspire to be like Christ; we must conform to His image and likeness that for the saints is the bounds of perfection. When we are righteous and holy, perfection is attainable.

We don't need to borrow from the blessing promises of the law; God gave Israel the power to get wealth through the law, but still, it was only a shadow of great things to come. He gave us the opportunity to be partakers of His divine nature. We don't need the spirit of Elijah when we are freely granted the Spirit of the Lord Jesus Christ directly from the Father. Through Christ the Lord, we partake in His divine nature. The more we become like Him, the more He wants us to become.

Dominion is in Christ, who is our life. We are called to be like Christ Jesus and work as joint heirs in His government. For as He is, so are we. I have no more time for boredom. I have too much living and growing to do.

All Scripture Quoted from Kings James Version

Printed in the United States
By Bookmasters